# SAUCY

**SAUCY**

Published by Nina Parker

November 2020
Published by Taylor Brothers Bristol Ltd, Units 5/6 Avon Valley
Business Park, Chapel Way, Bristol BS4 4EU

Text © Nina Parker
Photography © Kate Metzner, Juliana Parker (PVG Design) and Nina Parker 2020.
Design by Beth McCandlish (Monograph Design).
Printed and bound by Taylor Brothers, Bristol.

Cover image by Juliana Parker.

Published by Nina Parker, 2020
www.ninafood.com
@antoninaparker

ISBN 978-1-5272-7632-1

A proportion of each book sold will go towards financing tree
planting projects with environmental enterprise, Treecelet to neutralize
$CO_2$ emissions caused by production and shipping.

This publication has been printed on 400gsm Claro Silk and
150gsm Claro Gloss FSC® certified paperstocks, and is certified as
being produced carbon neutrally by the World Land Trust.

WORLD
LAND
TRUST™
www.carbonbalancedpaper.com
CBP004822

MIX
Paper from
responsible sources
FSC® C002762

# I LIKE IT SAUCY

What's the secret to eating well? For me it's all about giving your food a bit of sauce. So this is a book about sauce, because I believe the key to fuss-free, good food lies in a punchy dressing, marinade or salsa.

I have always eaten quite healthily, but 4 years ago I decided to go vegetarian for a month. I loved this new lifestyle and wanted to make it a permanent change. Although I liked the way this food made me feel, the day to day eating was sometimes a little dull. I realised that I needed to shake things up. I expanded my condiments cupboard and worked out that my crispy chilli oil tossed through noodles and dripped over rice bowls, could make the ordinary, extraordinary.

I am passionate about showcasing recipes that are healthy, but still full of flavour. This was an easy, quick way of injecting more spice into a simple dish. Let's be clear, I'm not talking about your traditional béchamels, peppercorns or hollandaise! Since my last books (Nina St Tropez and Nina Capri), I have scoured the world from California to Mexico and Japan, for some of the easiest, punchiest, jaw-droppingly delicious sauces, and brought them together into this book. I still keep to my roots and bring you a few Mediterranean ideas but, really this is a collection of over 100 recipes for the modern flexitarian. Whether you are cooking for one or a family, this book will vamp up everyday meals, dinner party dishes and desserts.

The book is divided into 6 chapters with specific recipe examples for each sauce. But feel free to make up your own fusions – the tiger bite or chilli sambal go well with a simple bowl of vegetables or fried egg. The mojo salsa makes an excellent topping for vegan tacos, or forget the pasta, and throw the roast pepper sauce on an avocado. I also highly recommend making a meal out of some of the sides for a tapas-style dinner that your guests will devour. Frankly, with great sauce at your fingertips, a last-minute fridge forage can be a thing of magic – cutting down on your food waste without cutting back on taste.

With the smaller size of the book, I wanted it to feel almost like a manual that you can take with you anywhere. And everyone who purchases this book, will also be giving back to our planet and to the environment. I am thrilled to be partnering up with environmental enterprise, Treecelet. With each book sold, a proportion of the profits will go towards replanting trees in Madagascar and will help in their efforts to educate and spread awareness about deforestation.

# ESSENTIAL INGREDIENTS

This is a list of ingredients that constantly feature throughout these recipes. My cupboard and fridge are always stocked up with the following:

## DRY

Chipotle paste

Gochujang paste

Toasted sesame oil

Apple cider vinegar

Soya sauce

Sunflower oil

Anchovies

**Mushroom powder**
(it's possible to blend dried porcini)

Shichimi seasoning

Dried chilli flakes

Onion powder

Garlic powder

Tahini paste

Sesame seeds

Vanilla extract

## FRESH

**White miso paste**
(for salad dressings)

**Brown miso paste**
(for roasting and frying)

Coriander

Lemons

Limes

Banana shallots

Garlic

Ginger

# CONTENTS

# BREAKFAST

# LUNCH

# DINNER

# EXTRAS

# PARTY

# SWEET

# BREAKFAST

These are my daily breakfasts throughout the week. Some are designed for when you have zero time but still need to get your fruit and vegetable intake. Other recipes include both of my famous spicy oils; Asian inspired chilli oil and crispy chilli oil. Although they are both designed to go with anything, they are incredible with eggs at the weekend.

# HISPI CABBAGE, EGG, ASIAN INSPIRED CHILLI OIL

This is a more intense version of the chilli oil from the scrambled tofu recipe. I re-vamped the recipe for a rainforest charity dinner that I hosted and it was such a hit on the night. People also went crazy for it during lockdown as it goes with ANYTHING! It's not very spicy, but it has depth of flavour. I would advise wearing gloves when chopping the chillies in case your hands are sensitive.

**VEGETARIAN | GF**

**Will make 600ml which is about two jars of chilli oil:**
6 mild chillies, deseeded and thinly sliced
3 banana shallots/1½ medium onions, thinly sliced
600ml sunflower oil
8 garlic cloves, diced
60g grated ginger
40ml sesame seed oil
80g brown miso paste

20g sesame seeds
A pinch of dried chilli flakes

**Serves 1**
½ hispi cabbage, sliced lengthways into 1cm thick, thick stalk removed
2 tbsp chilli oil
1 fried egg
Salt and pepper

Coriander for serving

For the chilli oil, weigh out and chop everything before you start. When I'm pushed for time, I use a blender to pulse blend the ingredients.

Add the sunflower oil to a large saucepan ensuring that there is at least a 5cm space from the top in case the oil spits. Slowly bring to a high heat. Add a small pinch of the chopped shallots to the oil and if it sizzles, you are ready to add the rest. Fry the shallots for about 6 minutes until they start to go a little golden. Then add the chopped chilli and fry for another 6 mins until they are starting to crisp up a little. Next, add the ginger and garlic and fry for 2 minutes. Keep watch as it can burn easily. The shallots should be quite crispy-looking by now. Remove the pan from the heat and leave for a bit to cool. Then add the miso paste, sesame oil, sesame seeds and a pinch of dried chilli. Store in a jar and when it's completely cooled keep in the fridge for weeks and weeks.

For the cabbage, set a frying pan on a medium to high heat and add a spoon of chilli oil. Then place the cabbage pieces into the pan to colour on one side. Use a spatula to press down to really char the edges for 1 minute. Then cover with a lid for 2 minutes before turning them over to do the same on the other side. Season with salt and pepper. Serve with chilli oil on top, a fried egg and coriander.

HISPI CABBAGE, EGG, ASIAN INSPIRED CHILLI OIL

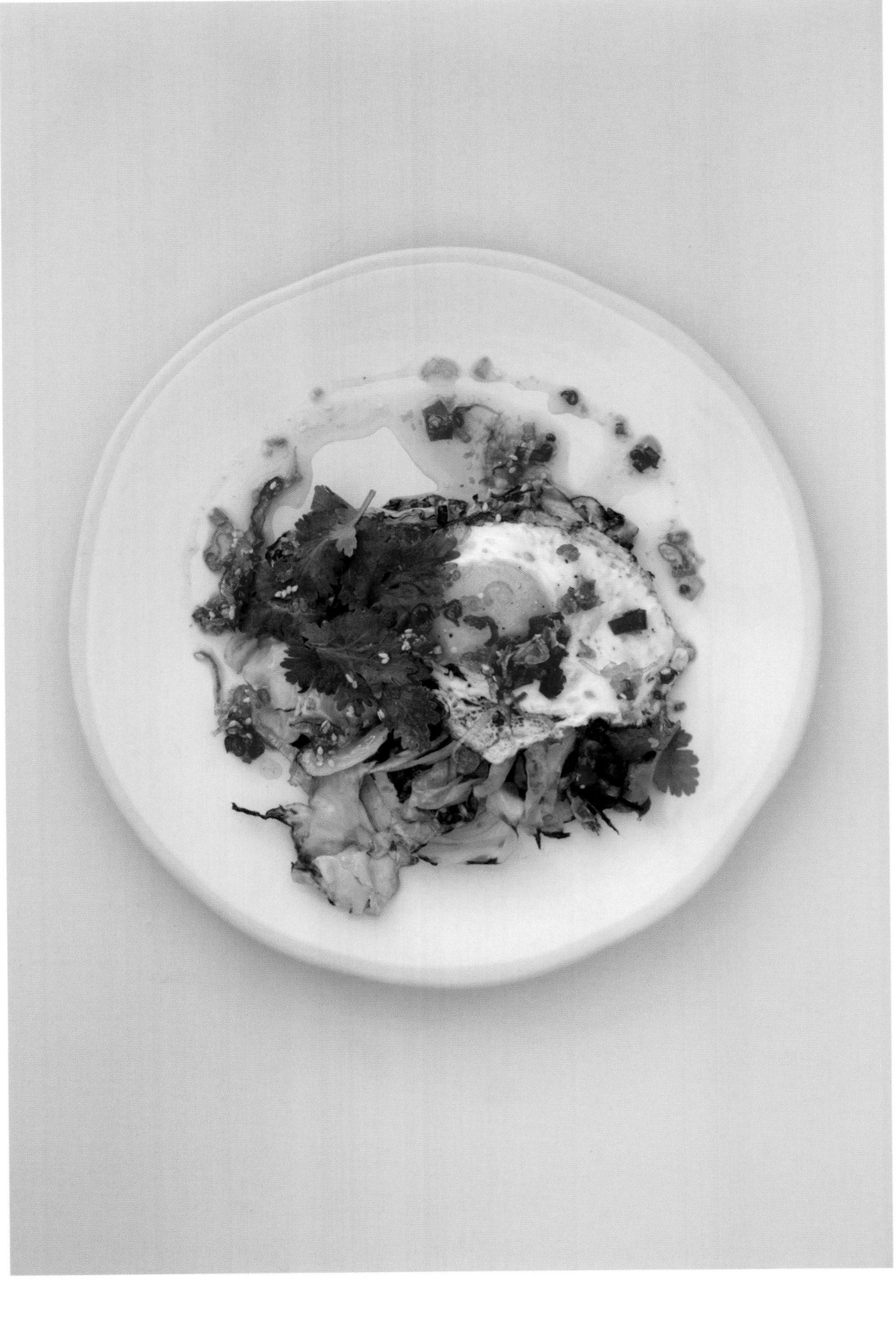

# RICOTTA TARTINE: TWO WAYS

---

One sweet, one savoury! Both excellent for brunch.

### Serves 1

### Honey & Blueberries
100g ricotta
Juice of half a lemon
1 tsp honey
½ tsp vanilla
100g blueberries (fresh or frozen)
1 slice of bread of your choice (I used spelt soughdough)

Add the ricotta to a bowl with a squeeze of lemon juice. Use a hand whisk to beat together for 20 seconds.

Set a frying pan on a medium to high heat and add the blueberries and a squeeze of lemon juice and the honey. Simmer everything together for 3 minutes and then add the vanilla. Remove from the heat.

Prep the toast with the ricotta spread on top and spoon over the blueberry compote and sauce.

### Serves 1

| Pomodorini Confit | For the confit (enough for 3) |
|---|---|
| 100g ricotta | 300g cherry tomatoes, halved |
| 1 tbsp extra virgin olive oil | 100g olive oil |
| 1 slice of bread of your choice | A few sprigs of thyme |
| | 1 tbsp dried oregano |
| | Salt and pepper |

Preheat the oven to 160°C degrees and line a large baking tray with baking parchment.

Add the tomato halves and cover in olive oil, thyme, oregano, salt and pepper. Bake in the middle of the oven for 40 minutes until shrivelled up and sweet. This keeps well in a jar in the fridge for 2 weeks.

Whip up the ricotta and olive oil with a hand whisk. Spread onto the toast and spoon over a few cherry tomatoes.

# EVERYDAY SMOOTHIE

I make a version of this 3-4 times a week! I love the fact that I can get a good dose of fruit in first thing and even though I make it all the time, I always look forward to it! I usually have it after my meditation and I always make double for my housemate, Carolina. We often chat about the plans for the day and catch up on any gossip, so it has a fun association for me. Swap with any seasonal fruit!

**VEGAN | GF**

**Serves 1**

2 handfuls of frozen fruits
½ frozen banana
3 tbsp oats
1 tsp chia seeds
A handful of almonds
A good pinch of cinnamon powder
2 tbsp coconut yoghurt
A few ice cubes

Throw everything into a high-speed blender and fill with cold water just below the top leaving about a 2cm gap. Whizz together for at least 30 seconds until smooth.

# PAN CON TOMATE

One summer, I reviewed a hotel in Majorca which had been converted from a beautiful, old farmhouse, called Finca Serena. Every morning for breakfast, they used to give you a pot of freshly crushed tomatoes grown from their kitchen garden. Sweet Spanish tomatoes paired with olive oil, sea salt and homemade bread is a hard combination to beat. I love the simplicity of this recipe and yet, the flavours are anything but. When tomatoes are in season, there is nothing better and this makes for a great breakfast. You can add a pinch of chilli or chipotle paste for an extra kick.

**VEGAN**

**Serves 1**

2 slices bread
150g cherry tomatoes (about a handful and a half)
2 tbsp extra virgin olive oil
Pinch of sea salt and black pepper
½ garlic clove

Put the bread slices in the toaster!

Add tomatoes, olive oil, salt and pepper into a blender and blitz until smooth. About 30 seconds or less. Do not over blend!

When the toast is ready, gently brush over the bread with garlic. Once is enough for a subtle flavour. Spread over the tomato paste, top with olive oil and serve!

# NASI GORENG

A Balinese classic! If you have leftover rice, this is what you have to make!

**VEGETARIAN | GF | DF**

**Recipe for 1**

2 tbsp sunflower oil/peanut oil
½ Chinese cabbage or ½ a small
white cabbage (white cabbage
takes a little longer to cook and
should be sliced on a mandoline)
1 medium carrot, grated
120g cooked short grain brown
rice (any rice works)
1 medium egg
½ spring onion, thinly sliced
Sriracha chilli sauce for
seasoning, optional
½ a sliced avocado and extra
lime for serving

**For the sauce**
3 tbsp soya sauce
1 tbsp galangal paste
A pinch of caster sugar
Zest and juice of half a lime

**For the paste (enough for 3 portions)**
1 banana shallot/1½ small shallots
½ lemongrass
½ thumb of ginger
1 big garlic clove
1 tsp tomato purée
A pinch dried chilli flakes
½ tsp caster sugar
15g peanuts

Begin by making the paste. Add all the paste ingredients to a blender and mix to a rough paste. Do not over blend! Scrape into a bowl and put to one side. This can be frozen or stored in an airtight container for 4 days in the fridge.

Prep all the vegetables. Set a large frying pan on a medium to high heat and add the oil followed by 3 tablespoons of the paste. Let this fry for about 3 minutes until the liquid from the paste starts to disappear and caramelise a little. Then add the cabbage as well as the carrot and fry for about 5 minutes. Finally add the rice and stir everything together.

While the cabbage fries, you can quickly mix together the sauce. Add all the ingredients together for the sauce and mix. Then pour this over the rice and cabbage and fry for 2-3 minutes. The rice will start to caramelise and crisp up a little. At this point, move the rice to one side of the pan and add a last splash of oil and crack the egg into the pan. Fry for about 2 minutes until cooked. Then plate up the rice with the egg on top followed by the avocado, spring onion, a drizzle of sriracha sauce and a slice of lime.

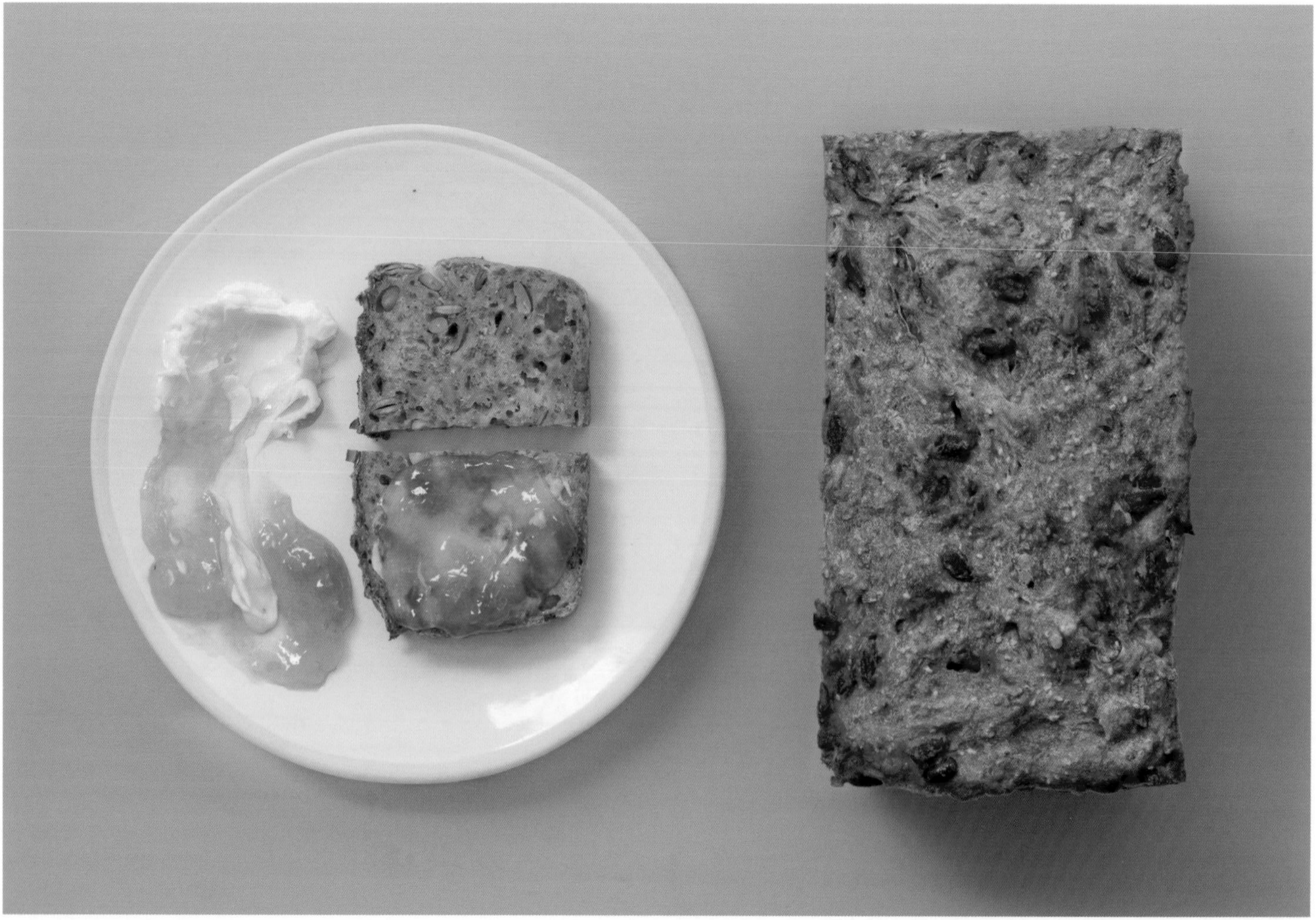

# CLAUDIA'S BEACH BREAD

This is such an easy, and seriously delicious loaf recipe. My sister's friend Claudia was kind enough to share it one summer when we were in the South of France. My family became obsessed with it because it is low in gluten and densely packed with nuts and seeds. You can swap around with these depending on what you have, and it makes an excellent vehicle for butter and apricot jam. I highly recommend making this when you have people to stay as it looks impressive but takes minimal effort!

**VEGAN | SPELT**

**Serves 6**

10g instant yeast
500g spelt flour
2 tbsp sunflower seeds
50g pine nuts
50g chia seeds
1 carrot, grated (90g)
2 tsp salt
2 tbsp apple cider vinegar
2 tsp vanilla extract
420-430ml lukewarm water

Preheat the oven to 200°C degrees.

Weigh and mix together all the dry ingredients including the carrots in a large bowl. Add the vinegar, vanilla extract and slowly mix in the water. It should come together easily into a sticky dough. Throw the dough into a buttered/greased standard loaf tin (900g/2lb) and place in the oven for about 1 hour or 1 hour 10 minutes. It should form a hard top and have come away from the edges slightly. Leave to cool for a few minutes before slicing up! This keeps for about 3 days covered in a cool, dry place.

# JOSH'S SPELT PANCAKES

My brother-in-law, Josh, makes pancakes every Sunday and I have to admit that he makes them better than I do. This is a version inspired by the amazing light pancakes that he makes using spelt flour. They have the thickness of an American style pancake but the size of a crêpe. Note, this is not exactly Josh's recipe because he does everything by eye and refuses to weigh anything.

### Makes 6-7 pancakes (enough for two)

180g spelt flour
2 medium eggs
320ml whole milk
½ tsp bicarbonate of soda
Pinch of sea salt
20g butter

### Fruit compote
100g cherries / any other seasonal berry
1 tsp sugar
Lemon juice
1 tsp maple syrup
Extra butter and maple syrup for serving

Sieve the flour, bicarbonate of soda and salt together. Then make a well and crack open the two eggs. Use a wooden spoon to combine together. When it starts to get a bit dry start adding in a little of the milk. Then beat to form a thick paste and get rid of any lumps. Continue adding in milk a little at a time until all is incorporated. It should be a thickish batter!

Set a frying pan to a medium to high heat and add some butter. When hot add 3-4 tbsp of the batter, moving the mix around the pan to create a largish pancake. Fry for about a minute until able to flip over. Fry on the other side for another minute until golden. Continue with the rest of the batter.

For the compote, add the ingredients to a saucepan and bring to a boil. Once bubbling, bring down to a simmer. Cook gently for about 10 minutes until the fruit has softened. Taste to check whether it needs a little more sugar before serving on top of the pancakes.

Josh's tip for the serving: When the pancake is ready, add a small knob of butter on top and a good splash of maple syrup that has been warmed in saucepan of hot water. This make all the difference, trust me!

ROAST SWEET POTATO, MEXICAN FLAVOURS, HOT SAUCE



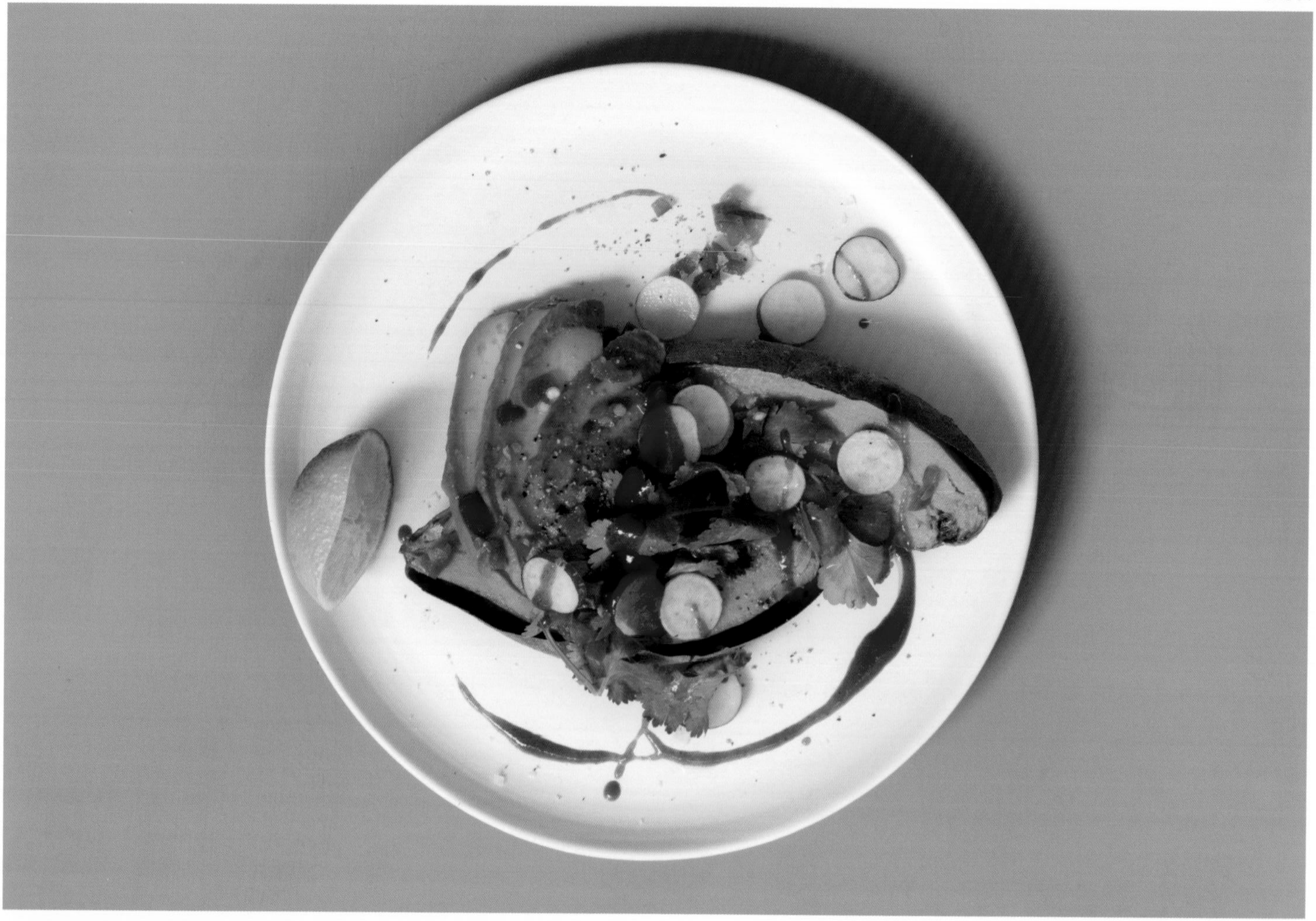

# ROAST SWEET POTATO, MEXICAN FLAVOURS, HOT SAUCE

---

I'm addicted to this set of flavours! Next time you are roasting sweet potatoes, add in a couple extra and you will have them ready to go or throw them in the oven while you get ready for work in the morning. I've kept this plant-based but you can always add an egg on top to bulk it up!

**VEGAN | GF**

**Serves 1**

1 medium-sized sweet potato
½ avocado, sliced
Handful of coriander leaves
1 tbsp pickled jalapeños, finely chopped
1 radish, thinly sliced
Squeeze of lime
Squeeze of sriracha

Prod the sweet potato a few times with a fork and roast in a 190°C degree oven for 25-30 minutes. Slice the sweet potato in half and load it up with everything! Drizzle over with sriracha.

# DATE TURMERIC SMOOTHIE

My sister, Juliana, got me into this. It's particularly good when you want an immunity boost!

**VEGAN | GF**

**Serves 1**

A large handful of almonds
2 large dates, pitted
1 thumb fresh turmeric
1 thumb fresh ginger
5 tbsp oats
4 ice cubes

Throw everything into a high-speed blender and top with cold water leaving about a 2cm gap from the top of the ingredients. You can always add more water to loosen if needed. Blend until smooth!

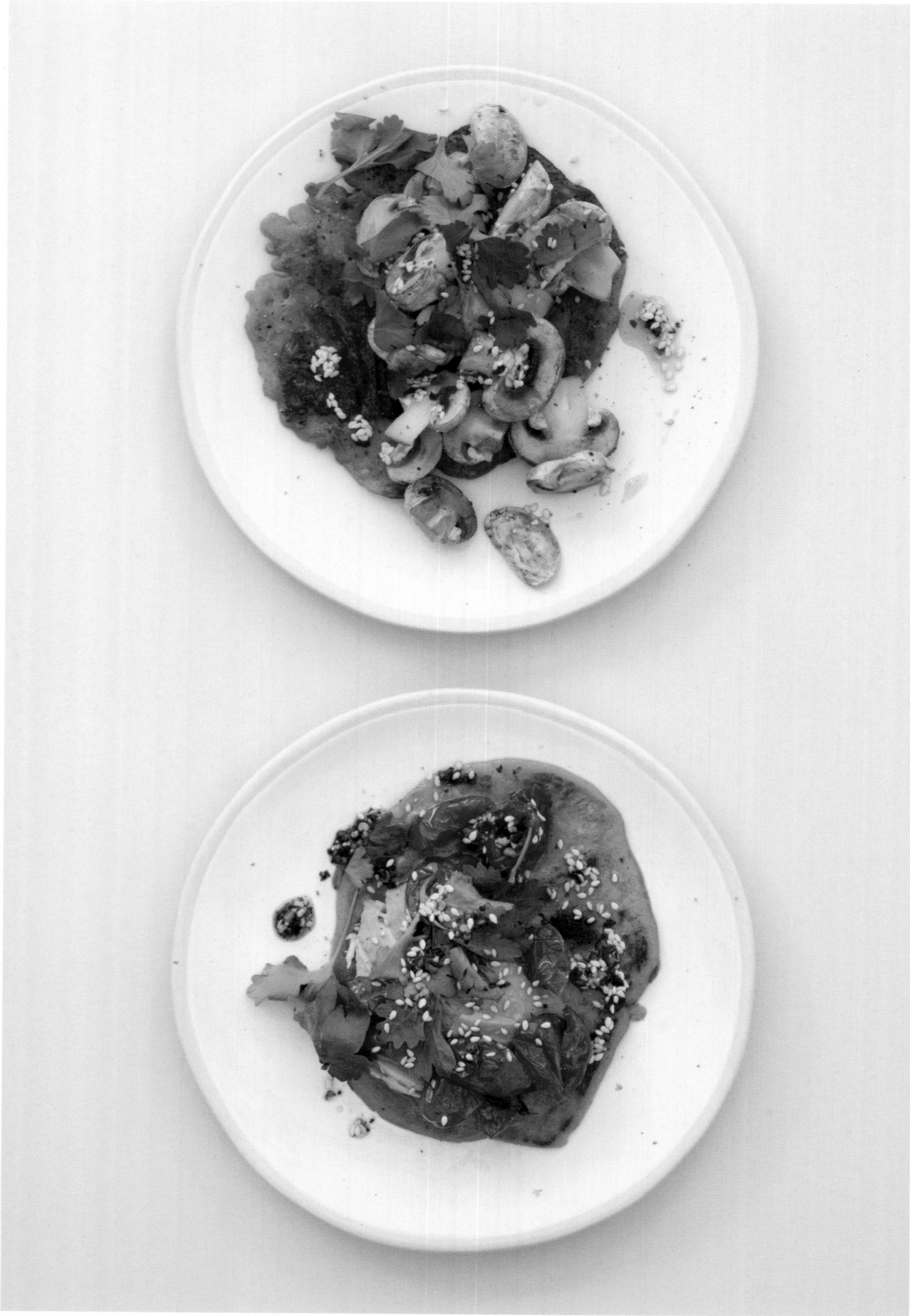

# SOCCA | QUICK HOT CHILLI OIL

Socca is a delicious kind of pancake made from chickpea flour and water originating from Nice in the South of France. It makes a great savoury breakfast.

**VEGAN | GF**

**Serves 2 (makes 4 pancakes)**

90g chickpea flour (sometimes called gram flour)
175ml cold water
1 tsp cumin powder
1 tsp turmeric powder
½ tsp salt
Black pepper
Sunflower/avocado oil for frying

**Quick Hot Chilli Oil**
200ml sunflower oil
5 tbsp dried chilli flakes
3 tbsp sesame seeds

**Toppings**
Fried mushrooms, Avocado, Cherry tomatoes, Fried egg, Tofu

In a large bowl add the chickpea flour and stir in the cold water getting rid of any lumps. Add the cumin, turmeric, salt and pepper. Leave to rest for 10-15 minutes to allow the mixture to thicken.

While the mixture rests, make your toppings!

Set a large non-stick frying pan on a medium to high heat and add a tablespoon of oil. Swirl this around the pan and use a ladle to make two pancakes. It's usually about 3 tablespoons of batter per pancake and leave them to fry until little air bubbles start to appear on top. Use a frying spatula to carefully flip them over and fry for another minute. They should be golden and a little crisp. Continue frying until all of the batter is finished. Serve with the toppings of your choice on top. They keep well the fridge for 2 days.

For the chilli oil, set a saucepan on a medium to high heat and add the oil. Allow this to heat up and then add the chilli flakes. Reduce the heat and allow the chilli to simmer for 1-2 minutes. Then add the sesame seeds and simmer for 1 minute before removing from the heat and leaving to cool. Store in a jar in the fridge for up to 3 weeks.

# RAPPER'S BANANA BREAD

I used to make this recipe all the time when I was grime artist Stormzy's private chef. After a few weeks, he asked me to stop making it because it was too addictive.

**SPELT**

**Serves 1**

110g unsalted butter, soft and cut into cubes
225g muscovado sugar
100g ground almonds
90g spelt flour
Pinch of sea salt
½ (level) tsp baking powder
½ (level) tsp bicarbonate of soda
2 (level) tsp cinnamon powder

100g dark chocolate, roughly chopped
350g ripe bananas for the batter (roughly 3) and then 1 banana halved for the top
85g buttermilk/milk with a few drops of lemon juice/plain yoghurt/soured cream
1 tsp vanilla extract
2 medium eggs, lightly beaten

Preheat the oven to 170°C degrees on the fan setting. Grease and line a standard loaf tin (900g/2lb) with baking parchment.

In a large mixing bowl, cream together butter and sugar. This will take about 5 minutes. Mix the dry ingredients together in a bowl (ground almonds, spelt flour, salt, baking powder, bicarbonate of soda and cinnamon powder). Mix in a little of the beaten eggs with the creamed butter, followed by a small amount of the dry ingredients. Make sure everything is incorporated before adding in more eggs and flour. Continue until both mixes are combined.

In a separate bowl, add the bananas, buttermilk and vanilla extract and use a fork to roughly mash everything together. Don't overmix and keep the mix a bit lumpy. Use a spatula to carefully fold this into the main batter. Then stir through the dark chocolate chunks. Do not overwork the mixture.

Scrape into the prepared tin and place into the oven for 40-45 minutes. Check at this point to see if the top is golden brown, then remove from the oven and cover the top with tin foil.

Place back in the oven for a further 15-20 minutes. It is ready when a skewer inserted comes out fairly clean but be warned, while it can look cooked from the outside, it will still need that extra 20 minutes after covering.

Leave to cool on a wire rack completely before dusting with a little cocoa powder. It lasts up to 4 days covered out of the fridge in a cool dry place.

# EGGS AND BEANS
# FROM MERCADO
# 28 DE NOVIEMBRE

I first heard about this market from one of my foodie heroes, Anthony Bourdain, when he ventured to this spot on his show "Parts Unknown". This was one of my first stops in Oaxaca City and I went back many times for spices and to try the famous drink of tejate. I understood how Bourdain must have felt, weaving in and out of the busy stalls, trying dried crickets and ordering a local breakfast. In true Mexican style, the market was colourful and there were some guitar players marching around. Even though this dish is unfussy, the beans were some of the best I've tasted with so much flavour and sauce. You tend to get a better sauce using tinned beans. You could swap this for fried tofu to make it plant-based!

### Serves 1

2 tbsp olive oil
180g tinned black beans, (keep some of the liquid)
1 tsp cumin powder
½ garlic clove, grated
½ tsp chipotle paste, optional
Salt and pepper
1 tsp butter
1 medium egg
½ chilli for serving

Set a saucepan on medium to high heat and add a tablespoon of olive oil followed by the garlic. Leave this to cook for 1 minute before adding in the black beans including some of the brown liquid from the tin, cumin powder, chipotle (if using) as well as salt and pepper. Fry for 1-2 minutes.

Set a frying pan on medium to high heat, add the butter and last spoon of olive oil. Let this melt before cracking the egg into the middle of the pan. Fry gently for about 3 minutes and reduce the heat halfway. Cook until a skin has formed on the yolk. Add to the beans along with some toast, chopped chilli or the Quick Hot Chilli Oil on page 41.

# BUCKWHEAT CRÊPES

These are delicate, slightly crispy pancakes. They are the perfect vehicle for a fruit compote or even a fried egg and chilli oil!

**VEGAN | GF**

**Serves 2/makes 6 crêpes**

120g buckwheat flour
1½ tsp ground flaxseed
½ tsp cinnamon powder
280ml unsweetened plant-based milk
1 tsp almond extract
3-4 tsp coconut oil/sunflower spread

**Toppings**
Almond butter
Coconut yoghurt
Fruit compote (taken from page 34)
Maple syrup

Add the flour, ground flaxseed and cinnamon to a bowl and mix together. Slowly stir in the milk followed by the almond extract until you have a thick batter.

Set a non-stick frying pan on a medium to high heat and add a teaspoon of coconut oil. When hot, add 2-3 tablespoons of the batter and swirl around the pan. Leave to fry without touching for 1½ minutes before using a spatula to flip over. Fry on the other side for the same amount of time and you should be left with slightly crispy sides. Flip onto a plate and continue making the rest.

Serve the crêpes with toppings!

# MAZUNTE
# SMOOTHIE BOWL

Smoothie bowls are nothing revolutionary if you have been on Instagram for the past few years, and yet, they only really hit me when I went to Mexico. When I was staying in San Agustinillo in the state of Oaxaca, I would often walk over to the next door, hippy beach town called Mazunte. This was where you could find live music, beach yoga, silent meditation retreats and the most delicious smoothie bowls. I became obsessed with creating my own concoctions depending on which fruit or supplement I wanted to add to the mix. This is a breakfast that should make you feel like you are on holiday. It certainly brings the sunshine!

**VEGAN | GF**

**Serves 1**

4 tbsp oats
1 tsp chia seeds
1 tbsp cashew nut butter
A good pinch of cinnamon
3 tbsp coconut kefir yoghurt
60g frozen blueberries
120ml almond milk
½ sliced frozen banana

**Toppings**
Desiccated coconut
Nuts
Bee pollen
Granola
Fresh fruit

Place all the ingredients for the smoothie into a blender and blend for at least 35 seconds until completely smooth. Pour into a bowl and top with a mix of toppings. Eat straight away!

# SCRAMBLED TOFU WITH CRISPY SHALLOT CHILLI OIL

I first tried scrambled tofu in an Ottolenghi restaurant with my wondrous pal, Sima. They did a Middle Eastern take with a citrus cucumber salad and this was a welcome change from having the usual scrambled eggs. Tofu is bland, there are no two ways about it but this chilli oil makes everything better.

**VEGAN**

**Serves 1**

160g silken tofu
100g mushrooms, thinly sliced and fried in batches without oil until golden
Handful coriander, roughly chopped
½ avocado, sliced
Few drops lemon/lime juice
2 tbsp chilli oil
1 toast

**For the crispy shallot chilli oil (makes about 1litre)**
260g banana shallots (about 6), thinly sliced widthways (you can use the same weight in red or white onions
200g mild chillies (about 12), sliced in half and deseeded, then thinly sliced
1 whole garlic (about 10 cloves), diced
800ml sunflower oil

For the chilli oil, prep all of your ingredients before you start frying. Then add the oil into a large saucepan and slowly bring the heat up. You can tell when the oil is hot enough when you add a slice of shallot into the pan and it sizzles. At this point, add the rest of the sliced shallots to fry for roughly 13-14 minutes or until they just start to colour and curl a little. The oil should be bubbling a little but not out of control. Then stir in the chopped chillies and fry for 7 minutes before adding in the chopped garlic. Cook for a further 2 minutes before removing from the heat. At this point the onions will have crisped up and the chillies will have started to curl and go a darker colour. If you are worried that it may continue to cook and burn after taking it off, you can add a bit more sunflower oil to help cool everything down and stop the cooking. Once cooled completely, store in a jar in the fridge for a month.

Set a large frying pan to a medium to high heat, add a tablespoon of the oil and use hands to crumble the tofu into the pan. Season generously with salt and pepper and use a spatula to move the tofu around so that it creates a scrambled egg texture. Scrape onto a toast and plate up with the sliced avocado, mushrooms, coriander, more chilli oil, a few drops of lemon or lime juice and a last seasoning.

# SKIN SMOOTHIE

When I'm feeling a bit run down and in need of a pick-me-up, this is it! It's probably half in my head but I always feel great after this smoothie. With a colour like this, how can it not be amazing for you?!

**VEGAN**

**Serves 1**

⅕ cucumber, peeled
⅓ avocado
A small bunch of coriander, including the stalks
⅓ of a green apple
A small handful of baby spinach
A good squeeze of lemon juice
½ thumb of fresh ginger
A handful of ice

Throw everything into a blender and fill almost to the top of the veg with cold water. You can always add more water. Blend until smooth. Drink straight away!

This is the chapter that gave me the inspiration for this book. I often make lunch at home and always look to eat a few of these veggie bowls a week. These dressings and sauces completely transform raw vegetables. They make lunches exciting and make you feel incredible. Not to mention, if you eat a few of these, it leaves room for some of the good stuff which can be found in the SWEET chapter. Get yourself the condiments from the Essential Ingredients list found at the beginning of the book and you will have these dressings on tap.

# BENTO BOX

I went to Japan for a work trip last year and I grabbed a bento box for the train from Tokyo to Izu. It was quite the experience to pick one as I had mostly no idea what was in each box, each one was a complete lucky dip. Whilst I spent about 20 minutes choosing a box, there were crowds all around me fiercely trying to grab their lunch as well as having numerous conversations with their work colleagues. It was overwhelming but amazing! I ended up choosing a crab, ginger and rice box which came with a wasabi dressing. I loved the concept of these neat lunches that were full of surprises. When I am at home, I like to create my own perfectly packed bento-style bowl. This is basically my lunch twice a week and I swap round with whichever veg is in season.

**VEGAN | GF**

**Serves 1**

80g cooked rice
50g silken tofu, sliced
Bunch of coriander, chopped once
Handful of mushrooms, sliced
½ an avocado, sliced
70g red cabbage, thinly sliced on a mandoline
1 tsp sesame seeds
⅓ red pepper, thinly sliced
½ black sesame seeds, optional
Bean sprouts, optional

**For the white miso dressing**
1 tsp white miso paste
3 tbsp lime juice
1 tbsp apple cider vinegar
½ tsp maple syrup
3 tbsp toasted sesame oil
1 tbsp water
Pepper and a little salt

In a small bowl, whisk all the ingredients for the dressing together and taste to check the seasoning.

Prep all the salad ingredients and tuck neatly into a serving bowl. Pour the dressing over and serve with some lime on the side.

# PLACE DU SUD SALAD WITH ANCHOVY DIJON VINAIGRETTE

Lunchtime in the South of France is about a handful of delicious, seasonal ingredients and knocking them together with a no-fuss but punchy dressing. This is La Sauce!

**GF**

**Serves 1**

**Optional ingredients**
1 baby gem lettuce, torn
A handful of lamb's lettuce
Half an avocado, sliced
A handful of blanched green beans, halved
A handful of cherry tomatoes, halved
1 boiled egg, halved

**Dressing**
1 anchovy, chopped and mashed into a paste
2 tbsp red wine vinegar
1 tsp Dijon mustard
3 tbsp extra virgin olive oil
Salt and pepper

Prep all the vegetables for the salad and place into a bowl.

Add the anchovy paste to a small bowl and whisk in the vinegar, mustard, salt and pepper. Then slowly whisk in the olive oil to create an emulsion. Drizzle over the salad and eat straight away!

# MEXICAN INSPIRED RICE BOWL

I love using chipotle paste for simple lunchtime dressings as it really vamps up even the humblest salad. The smokey, sweet hum from these Mexican chillies takes me straight back to the markets in Oaxaca City where I brought a bucket full of dried varieties back to make moles. This is a quick vinaigrette that I turn to again and again and although you can use whatever you have, I insist you go the whole hog, and give it a Mexican feel. Leave out the egg to make this plant-based!

**Serves 1**

½ soft avocado
Handful cherry tomatoes, halved
3 tbsp cooked rice (I used short grain brown rice)
3 baby corn/large handful of cooked frozen corn
1 7-minute boiled medium egg, sliced in half
60g cooked black beans
Handful greens (I used baby spinach)
Handful coriander, roughly chopped
1 tbsp sprouts
1 lime
1 tbsp olive oil

**Chipotle dressing**
1½ tsp chipotle paste (depending on the heat)
3 tbsp olive oil
1 tsp maple syrup
3 tbsp lime juice and a bit of zest
Salt and pepper

Prep all the veg and cook the egg. If using baby corn, blanch for 3 minutes in boiling water and drain.

Mash the avocado with a fork in a bowl, add the juice of half a lime, a tablespoon of olive oil and a pinch of salt.

Mix all the ingredients for the dressing together into a bowl and taste to check the seasoning is good.

Plate up everything. Drizzle over the dressing and serve with a wedge of lime on the side!

# L'ESCALET PICNIC SALAD WITH GINGER LIME DRESSING

When I was in the South of France, my family and I took a picnic to l'Escalet which is about a 25-minute drive from our house. This beach has amazing swimming and the landscape is completely unspoilt. I brought this salad along which was more delicious than I had expected as the fried carrots added in the "je ne sais quoi".

**VEGAN | GF**

**Recipe for a greedy 2**

150g chickpeas (cooked)
1 red pepper, diced
100g cherry tomatoes, halved
2 medium carrots, diced
1 courgette, sliced with a mandoline
A handful of flat leaf parsley leaves
4 tbsp olive oil
70g cashews
1 avocado, diced (optional)

**For the ginger lime dressing**
3 tbsp toasted sesame oil
3 tbsp white wine vinegar
2 tbsp tamari soya sauce
3 tbsp lime juice (about ½ a juicy lime)
1 level tbsp grated ginger
A small pinch of sugar
Black pepper

Add the ingredients for the dressing together in a small bowl and mix. Taste to double check the seasoning. Add the prepped diced pepper, chickpeas, flat leaf parsley and cashews into a large bowl. Set a frying pan to a medium to high heat and add two tablespoons of oil. Then add the diced carrots with a pinch of salt and pepper and fry for about 2-3 minutes until they have softened a little. Add the carrots to the bowl and add another bit of oil to the frying pan. Use the mandoline to slice the courgette straight into the hot pan. Cook for about 2 minutes until golden on both sides. Add this to the bowl and mix in along with the dressing. Add some black pepper to finish and throw in some avocado if you fancy.

# LENTIL SALAD WITH A MAPLE CHIPOTLE DRESSING

This is a great salad to take to work and holds together even if you dressed it in the morning. You can add whichever vegetables you like, but definitely get into the habit of adding in the pickles. Chipotle goes so well with lentils as it has a smokey flavour that is found in chorizo which is also a good pairing for them.

**VEGAN | GF**

**Serves 2**

1 large handful flat leaf parsley leaves
160g dried small green lentils
1 vegetable stock cube
2 pinches salt
200g broccoli spears, blanched in boiling water
for 3 minutes then roughly chopped
250g tomatoes, deseeded and then cut into little
cubes/cherry tomatoes, halved
1 red pepper, deseeded and then cut into little cubes
50g small white pickled onions, thinly sliced
100g sun-dried tomatoes, roughly chopped

**For the dressing**
2-3 level tsp chipotle paste (depending on how hot the paste is)
½ garlic clove, grated
5 tbsp extra virgin olive oil
Zest of 1 lemon and 6 tbsp lemon juice
1 tbsp balsamic vinegar
1 tsp maple syrup
Salt and black pepper

In a small bowl, mix everything together for the dressing and check the seasoning.

Rinse the lentils under cold water for 1 minute and transfer into a large saucepan. Cover the lentils with cold water ensuring there is an additional 4cm of liquid. Crumble in the stock cube and add the salt. Bring to the boil and then down to a simmer. Check the packet's instruction but the small variety should take about 20-22 minutes. Drain and either serve warm if eating straight away or allow the lentils to cool before mixing in the rest of the ingredients. Pour over the dressing and taste to check the seasoning.

# GRUB'S GREEN GODDESS SALAD

My friend Grubbage likes to make this dressing for lunch and he generously shared it with me over a pint in Notting Hill. Since trialing it out I have noticed that it also makes a good dipping sauce for nachos and bread. You definitely have to love avocado for this one and it gives the dressing this wonderful silky-smooth texture. You even get a helping of raw spinach thrown into the mix. For this textured dressing, I would pair it with salmon, chicken or chunky textures with lettuce.

**VEGAN | GF**

**Serves 1**

**Optional salad idea**
1 baby gem lettuce
2 handfuls of finely chopped kale
2 radishes, thinly sliced
Handful roasted carrots or any roast vegetable
¼ fennel bulb, shaved with a mandoline
Spelt croutons (use whatever you have)
1 tbsp sunflower seeds
Zest of ½ a lemon

**Dressing**
⅓ avocado
Small handful cashews
Half a handful baby spinach
3½ tbsp extra virgin olive oil
2 tbsp apple cider vinegar
Pinch chilli flakes
4-5 tbsp cold water
2 tbsp lemon juice
Salt and pepper

Add all the dressing ingredients together into a blender. Blitz to a smooth consistency and add to a bowl. Taste to check the seasoning.

Prepare the salad in a bowl and pour the dressing on top. Season with salt, pepper, lemon zest and a last drizzle of extra virgin olive oil.

# RAW RAINBOW, LEMON CASHEW DRESSING

---

I use cashew butter to create a creamy vinaigrette with fresh ginger and lemon. You can use whatever raw veg you have in the fridge, but the main thing is having a good grater and you'll whip it up in less than ten minutes. I used to think slaw was rubbish, but this is damn good!

**VEGAN | GF**

**Serves 2**

1 medium beetroot, grated
½ fennel, thinly sliced with a mandoline
80g kale, finely chopped and rubbed together with hands
to reduce in size
2 handfuls of spinach, chopped
100g chickpeas
1 avocado, thinly sliced
2 medium carrot, grated
1 tbsp sesame seeds
¼ white/red cabbage, thinly sliced
Handful cashews, roughly chopped

**For the dressing**
4 tbsp cold water
2 tbsp toasted sesame oil
3 tbsp cider/white wine vinegar
3 tbsp soya sauce
1½ tbsp freshly grated ginger
1 tsp maple syrup
Zest of 1 lemon, 4 tbsp juice
3 tbsp cashew nut butter
Black pepper

Add all the ingredients for the dressing together in a small bowl and whisk until combined. Taste to check the seasoning, adding in more pepper or even some extra salt.

Add all the chopped veg into a bowl and toss together with dressing.

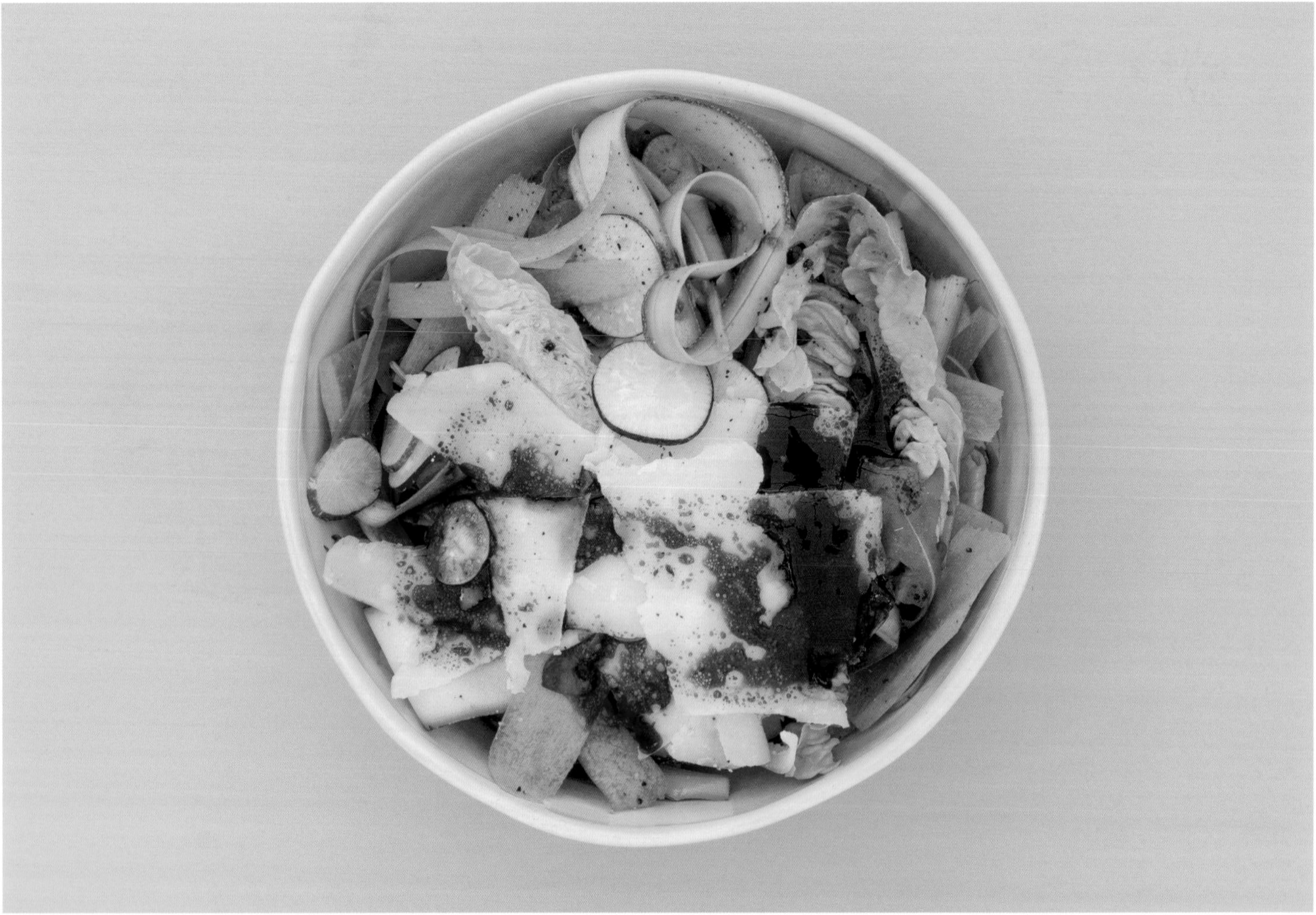

# SALINS SALAD | TRUFFLE BALSAMIC

Just outside St Tropez there is an incredible restaurant called la Plage des Salins that sits on the beach with blue parasols, rocky coves and the most incredible sunsets. There are a few beach houses that I always admire when I visit, but I pay particular attention to a modern, Palm Springs-style bungalow that sits on this waterfront. The restaurant has been around for many years and offers tuna salads and nems (spring rolls) for lunch and wood-fired pizzas for dinner. There is something special about this spot and I love it for its effortless charm and rustic, laidback style. My niece, Ines and nephew, Phoenix always go for the pork spring rolls wrapped in lettuce with fresh mint with a sweet chilli dip. My sister and I often grab this raw vegetable salad with shavings of parmesan and truffle balsamic vinaigrette. Just the thought of this reminds me of the good times, getting off the hot beach and into the shade to enjoy this with a glass of rosé in hand.

**VEGETARIAN | GF**

**Serves 1**

20g shaved parmesan, cut with a peeler
A mix of the following vegetables thinly sliced with a mandoline:
carrot, courgette, asparagus
Handful of rocket
Baby gem lettuce
1 tbsp sunflower seeds
Small handful walnuts, crumbled

**For the dressing**
3 tbsp truffle olive oil
2 tbsp aged balsamic (or any kind)
Salt and black pepper

Prep all the veg and add to a bowl. Mix the dressing ingredients together into a bowl and taste to check the seasoning. Pour over the salad and serve!

# SESAME HONEY HALLOUMI, SALAD, LEMON DRESSING

I first had fried halloumi in a little taverna on the island of Kefalonia in Greece. They served it with a generous squeeze of lemon juice that completely elevated it. Here I have added honey and sesame to the mix.

**VEGETARIAN | GF**

**Serves 1**

1 baby gem
A handful of rocket
1 tomato, sliced
½ avocado, sliced

**For the halloumi**
2 tbsp olive oil
2 thick 2cm slices of halloumi
1 tbsp honey, plus extra for garnish
1 tbsp sesame seeds
1 tsp nigella/black sesame seeds
A few drops of lemon juice

**Dressing**
2 tbsp extra virgin olive oil
1 tbsp toasted sesame oil
⅓ tsp honey
2 tbsp white wine vinegar
2 tbsp lemon juice
Salt and pepper

Prep your salad in a bowl and mix the dressing together!

Set a frying pan on a medium to high heat and add the olive oil for the halloumi. Season the cheese generously with pepper and add the slices to the hot pan. Fry for 2 minutes until the bottom starts to go golden and then flip them over. Drizzle half the honey over the golden sides while they cook on the other side. Once the other side is crispy and golden, turn them over and add the remaining honey on top. Fry for another 1 min which should let the honey caramelise a little. Pour half the seeds onto a plate and press the slices on top, sprinkling the rest on the other side. Drizzle over a little extra honey along with sea salt and squeeze over the lemon juice. Dress the salad and serve slices on top to eat straight away.

# ROAST SUMMER VEGETABLES WITH TAHINI POMEGRANATE SAUCE

A favourite from my food series with Millie Mackintosh.

**VEGAN | GF**

**Serves 2**

100g asparagus, ends trimmed
350g carrots, peeled, topped and
tailed, sliced into uneven sticks
of about 1cm thick
1 medium aubergine,
sliced into even wedges
½ broccoli, divided into equal florets
100g cherry tomatoes, halved
Handful flat leaf parsley leaves
200g cooked chickpeas
6 tbsp olive oil
A few pinches of Aleppo chilli, optional
3 tsp sumac

**For the dressing**
4 tbsp tahini paste
2 tbsp toasted sesame oil
8 tbsp lemon juice and the zest
of a lemon plus x2 tbsp more juice
4 tbsp apple cider vinegar or
white wine vinegar
2½ tbsp pomegranate molasses
¼ tsp grated garlic
Sea salt and black pepper
Some cold water to loosen the
tahini paste

Preheat the oven to 190°C degrees and line 2-3 baking trays with baking parchment. Put the chopped carrots into a bowl and add 2 tbsp olive oil, a tsp sumac, salt and pepper. Mix everything together and tip into the baking tray, spreading them out evenly. Then add the aubergine into the bowl and do the same followed by the broccoli. Season with sumac, Aleppo chilli if using and olive oil. Make sure that each vegetable is laid out separately as they will have slightly different cooking times. Then coat the asparagus and cherry tomatoes with olive oil, salt and pepper and add to the trays. Put all the trays into the oven and leave for 10-12 minutes. The asparagus should be cooked by now so remove from the oven. Then continue to roast everything for another 10 minutes and remove the broccoli if it is soft. Then roast again for another 10 and the aubergine, carrots and cherry tomatoes should be done. Add all of the vegetables together into a bowl and add the parsley leaves, chickpeas and a few more pinches of sumac.

In a bowl, add all of the ingredients together for the dressing and whisk together. I add a little cold water to loosen the tahini if it is a little hard to mix. Taste and check the seasoning is to taste. Serve with the sauce in a little bowl on the side.

# LA MAKE OUT SALAD

---

Matthew Kenney has made waves with his LA plant-based restaurants and "Make Out" is no different. He is creative when it comes to plants and has some seriously beautiful plates of food. It is like fine-dining for vegans! I had something called the Make Out Salad when I was there and this is in the spirit of his food. Soft lettuce, avocado, thinly shaved raw veg, nuts and seeds work well with this dressing. You can use one mustard if that is all you have although the Dijon and grainy work well together. You can even swap to a hot mustard for more of a kick. Ground hempseed is amazing sprinkled over salads and an excellent source of protein, also containing omega 3 and 6.

**VEGAN | GF**

**Serves 1**

½ butter lettuce/chopped baby gem lettuce
80g thinly sliced cabbage (I use a mandoline)
Large handful baby spinach
Handful chopped coriander
½ avocado, sliced
1 tbsp ground hempseed
1 tbsp pumpkin seeds

**Mustard dressing**
3 tbsp extra virgin olive oil
½ tsp Dijon mustard
½ tsp grainy mustard
1 tbsp red wine vinegar
Zest of half a lemon and 1 tsp lemon juice
⅓ tsp honey
1 tbsp diced shallot (run under cold
water for 1 minute in a sieve)
Salt and black pepper

Prep the salad in a bowl.

In a small bowl, mix all the ingredients together for the dressing and taste to check the seasoning. It should be sharp with a slight balance of sweet. Pour over the salad and serve!

The dressing keeps well in a jar in the fridge for 5 days.

DINNER

This is the largest chapter which pays homage to my travels and is filled with stories from Mexico City to Lisbon and back to London working as Stormzy's private chef. Some of these require a little more time, usually in the form of roasting. You will find noodles, curries and a range of good pasta sauces. I cannot recommend the roast red pepper sauce with pangrattato enough! These dishes provide comfort as well as flavour and I have offered ideas for different seasons.

# ROAST PEPPER SAUCE, PANGRATTATO PASTA

This sauce is a mix between a romesco sauce and an incredible pasta that I ate at my favourite London restaurant, Pophams. They served a peppery sauce with breadcrumbs. I love using up stale bread to make breadcrumbs and this compliments the pasta, adding in lots of texture. I usually like to sprinkle them on a Puglia-style broccoli pasta but I think this might be a better combination.

**VEGAN**

**Serves 2**

**For the pangrattato**
3 handfuls stale bread
3 tbsp olive oil
½ tsp garlic powder
Salt and pepper

**For the roast pepper sauce**
440g red peppers (I use a mix of bell and romano), thinly sliced and deseeded
4 tbsp olive oil, plus 70ml extra virgin olive oil

2 banana shallots, sliced
3 garlic cloves, sliced
1½ tsp ground paprika
Few sprigs of thyme
100g cherry tomatoes, halved
½ tsp cayenne pepper
Zest of 1 lemon and 3 tbsp lemon juice
Salt and pepper
200g pasta of your choice
(rigatoni pictured)

For the pangrattato, blend the stale bread to a rough consistency, leaving some chunky bits. Add to a baking tray and drizzle over the olive oil, garlic powder, salt and pepper. Place into a 190°C degree preheated oven for 4-5 minutes until crisped up and golden. Leave to cool and store in a jam jar.

For the sauce, preheat the oven to 190°C degrees and line two baking trays with baking paper. Add the sliced peppers to one and season with 2 spoons of olive oil, salt and pepper. Then add the onions, thyme leaves, garlic and tomato halves to the other and season with another two spoons of olive oil, salt and pepper. Place both trays into the oven. Take out garlic and thyme at 12 minutes, the onion at 20 and the rest at 30. Scrape this into a blender along with 30ml of olive oil, paprika and cayenne pepper. Blend to a smooth consistency and add to a bowl. Add the lemon zest, juice, remaining olive oil and season. Serve with the pasta of your choice using some of the starchy water to loosen the sauce. Top with pangrattato!

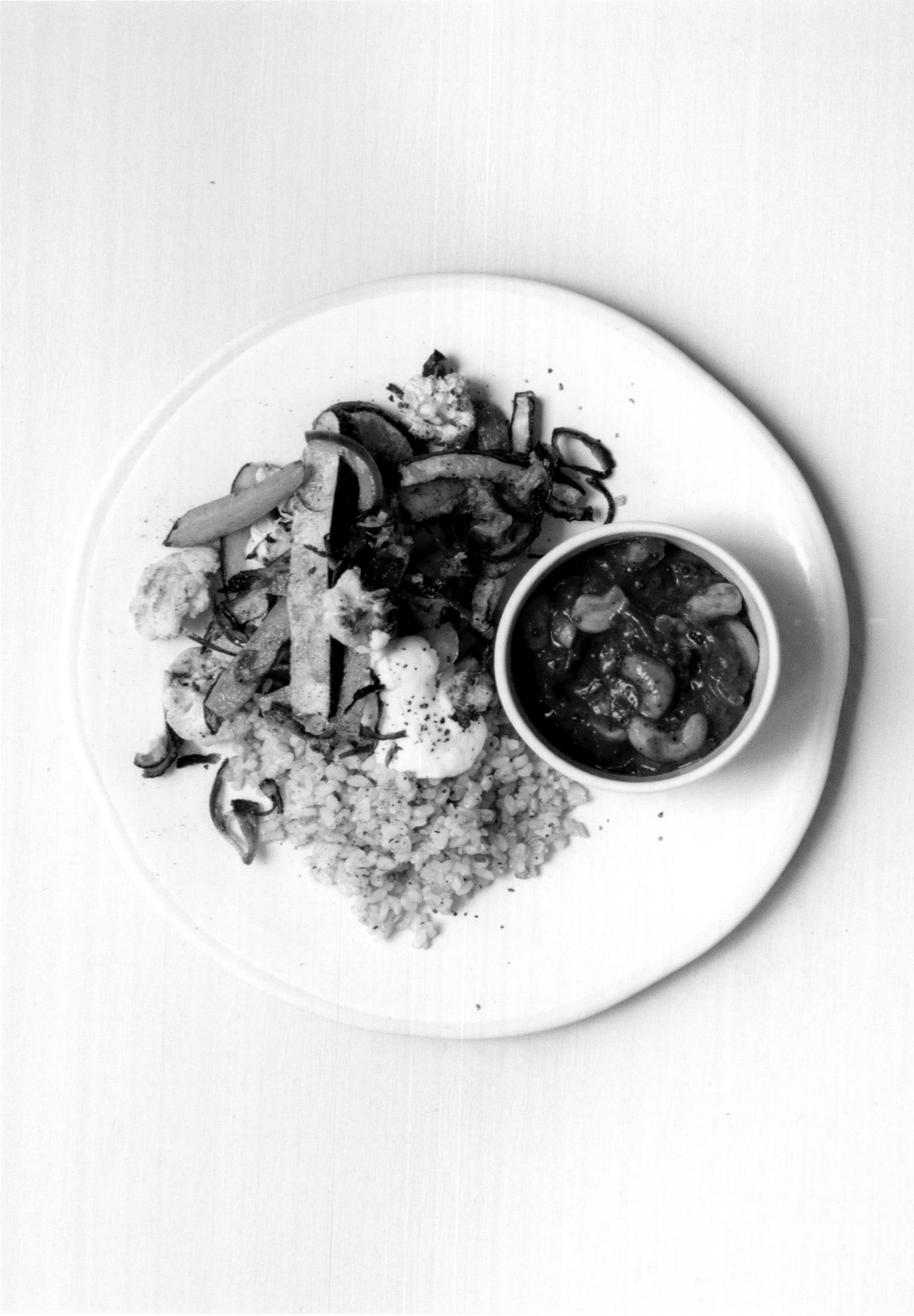

# MUMBAI NIGHTS

I feel as though I have only touched the tip of the iceberg when it comes to Indian cuisine. I spent 4 nights wandering around Mumbai before heading to Goa and Kerala. On my last night, I went to a rooftop restaurant covered in pastel coloured canopies and devoured a prawn vindaloo. This sauce is not as spicy, but it is a dedication to the aromatic tomato, coconut, mustard seed fusion that I had on my last night overlooking the vibrant city. You can use most vegetables for this recipe as long as you keep to this spice palette.

**VEGAN | GF**

**Serves 2**

2 carrots, cut into 1cm thick sticks
1 courgette, cut into 1cm thick sticks
½ cauliflower, cut into florets
½ red onion, thinly sliced
4 garlic cloves, diced
1 tsp coriander powder
1 tsp cumin powder
1 tsp turmeric powder
3 tbsp coconut oil, melted
Salt and pepper

**For the sauce**
2 tbsp coconut oil
1 red onion, thinly sliced
1 tbsp mustard seeds
½ tsp dried chilli flakes
100g cherry tomatoes, halved
1 tbsp tomato purée
120ml coconut cream
70g cashews
Juice of ½ a lime

Preheat the oven to 190°C degrees fan and line a baking tray with baking parchment. Arrange chopped vegetables in the tray and season with chopped garlic, the 3 spices, coconut oil, salt and pepper. Place into the oven to roast for 20 minutes and remove the courgette. Toss everything around the pan and bake for another 10 minutes.

While the vegetables are roasting, you can make the sauce. Set a large saucepan on a medium to high heat and add the coconut oil. Let this heat up for a minute and add the chopped onion. Fry for 2 minutes before adding in the mustard seeds and chilli flakes. Cook for 1 minute and then add cherry tomatoes and tomato purée. Stir everything around and reduce the heat to a simmer. Cover with a lid leaving a small gap for the steam to escape. Simmer for 5 minutes and then add the coconut cream, cashews and season with salt and pepper. Bring back to a boil for 30 seconds to allow the flavours to infuse and remove from the heat. Mix in the lime juice and serve with the roast vegetables and rice.

# ROMA NORTE STEW, CHIPOTLE OIL

Roma Norte is probably my favourite part of Mexico City. It's a district full of amazing restaurants, coffee shops and colourful residential houses with jacaranda trees in full purple bloom. I will never forget wandering around the streets with a taco in hand listening to the iconic birds chorus. I had about three different versions of this stew in various markets and restaurants. You are often served a simple chipotle oil on the side to add to tacos and tostadas. The oil elevates this humble one-pot quick dinner!

**VEGAN | GF**

**Serves 2**

1 medium onion, diced
1 celery stick, diced
1 medium carrot (200g), diced
4 garlic cloves, diced
4 tbsp olive oil
180g medium tomatoes, roughly chopped
500ml hot vegetable stock
200g black beans, cooked
1 tbsp chipotle paste
Salt and pepper

**Toppings**
1 avocado, sliced
A small bunch of coriander, roughly chopped
160g cooked rice
Zest and juice of 1 lime
2 tbsp pickled jalapeños, chopped

Set a large saucepan on a medium to high heat and add two tablespoons of olive oil. Then add the onion, celery and carrot to fry for 3 minutes. Stir in the diced garlic and fry for 1 minute before adding in the tomatoes to cook for 2 minutes. Pour in the hot vegetable stock and bring to a boil and then down to a simmer for 3 minutes. Add the beans and season with salt and pepper.

In a small bowl mix together the remaining olive oil and chipotle paste. Serve the stew in bowls with the avocado, rice, coriander and jalapeños on top! Drizzle the chipotle over and serve with half a lime on the side!

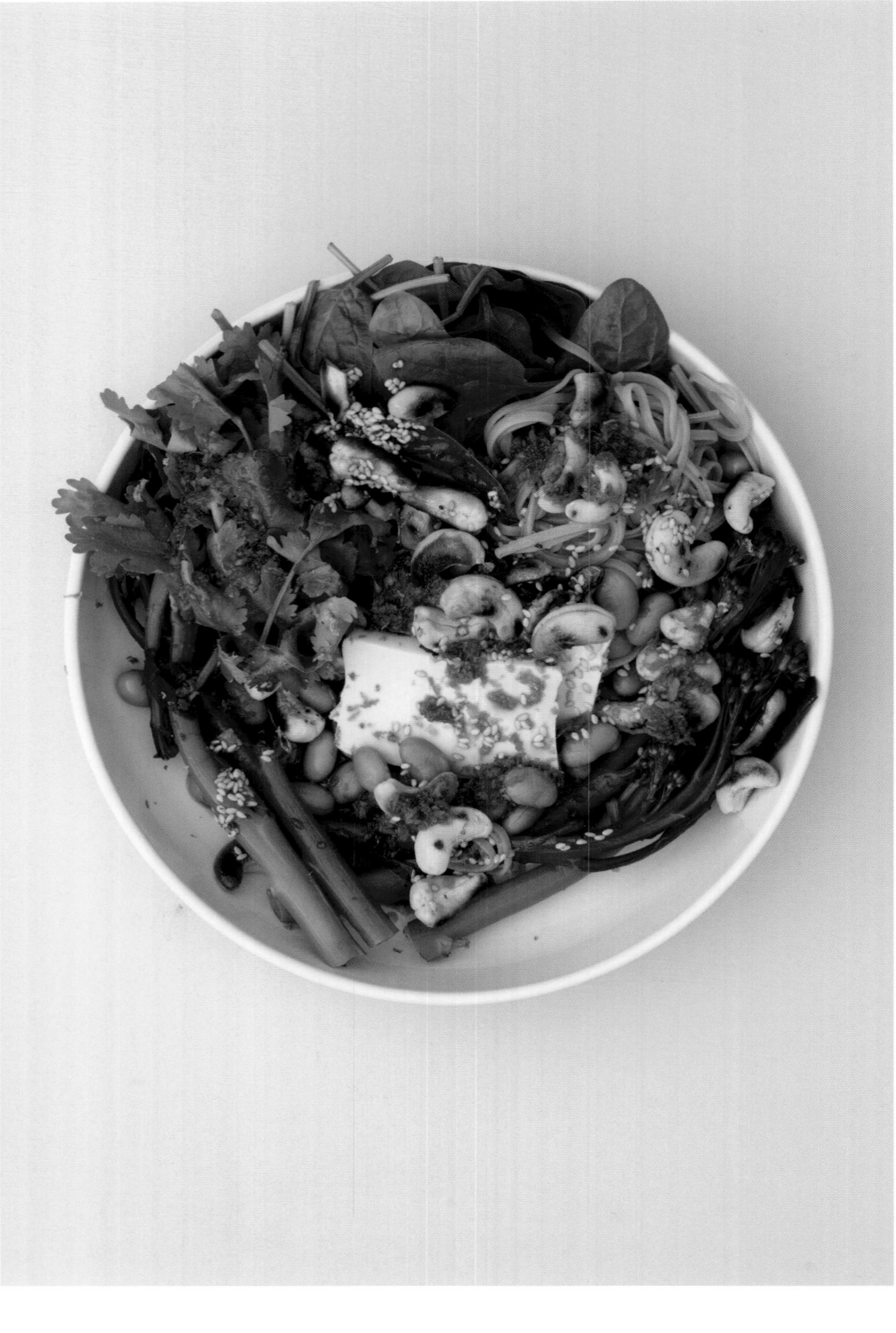



NOODLE SALAD, GREENS, TERIYAKI AND SPICY CASHEWS

# NOODLE SALAD, GREENS, TERIYAKI AND SPICY CASHEWS

I encourage you to make a batch of the spicy cashews to sprinkle over salads. They really light things up and provide some good texture.

**VEGAN | GF**

**Serves 2**

200g cooked soba noodles/brown rice (served cold)
160g silken tofu, sliced
3 handfuls of spinach, chopped
2 handfuls of coriander, chopped
80g edamame beans (I used frozen)
100g broccoli, blanched in boiling water for 3 minutes

**For the teriyaki sauce**
9 tbsp soya sauce
9 tbsp white wine vinegar
3 level tsp sugar

2½ level tbsp grated and finely chopped ginger
1 garlic clove, grated

**For the spicy cashews**
100g cashews
5 tbsp sunflower oil
3 pinches of dried chilli
Pinch of salt
2 tbsp sesame seeds
(You'll only need 30g for the recipe but it's nice to make extra for other salads)

Boil a kettle and add the edamame to a bowl. Then pour the boiled water over the bowl. Leave for a couple of minutes and then drain.

Prep the other vegetables.

Add the cashews to a frying pan and set on a high heat. Let them colour on one side for 30 seconds or so and then add the sunflower oil, sesame seeds, salt and chilli. Turn down the heat a little and allow everything to mix and infuse together. Remove when the cashews are lightly golden. Roughly chop a few handfuls for the salad and store the rest in a jar.

Put the ingredients for the teriyaki sauce in the same frying pan and bring to the boil. Then simmer for 1 minute and remove from the heat.

Assemble the salad and drizzle over the teriyaki and chopped cashews on top.

# LAST OF THE SUMMER ROOFTOP PARTY CANNELLINI BEAN STEW

I made this for a late September rooftop party at my wonderful mate Casty's house. Everybody brought a dish and there may have been a drone. This is a Tuscan-style soup and it is made even more special with my classic chilli oil with shallots found on page 50.

**VEGETARIAN | GF**

**Serves 2**

6 tbsp olive oil
1 white onion, diced
1 medium carrot, roughly chopped
into small pieces
4 sticks celery, roughly chopped
into small pieces
4 garlic cloves, diced
200g butternut squash, roughly
chopped into small pieces

100ml white wine
1 tbsp tomato purée
900ml hot vegetable stock
250ml cooked cannellini beans
½ tsp cumin powder
A bunch of sage leaves
Sea salt and black pepper
Zest of a lemon and the juice of half
3-4 tbsp ricotta cheese

Set a large saucepan on a medium to high heat and add 4 tablespoons of the olive oil. Add in the onion and celery and allow them to cook for 3 minutes before adding in the diced garlic, cooking that for 1 minute. Then add in the carrot, squash and tomato purée. Mix everything together, pouring in the white wine and allow the flavours to infuse and the alcohol to cook off for 2 minutes. Pour over the hot stock bringing the pan to the boil and then down to a gentle simmer for 10 minutes or so until all the veg is cooked through.

While the veg is cooking, set a frying pan on a medium to high heat and add the remaining olive oil. Then add the sage leaves to fry for a minute until just cooked and the sage is crispy. Stir in the cannellini beans and cumin powder into the soup and season with salt, pepper and the lemon zest and juice. You can blitz a little of the mix in a blender if you want to thicken it, but I left mine chunky. Serve with the crispy sage on top, a dollop of ricotta and if you have it handy, some chilli oil!

# BIGOLI IN SALSA

I ate this in Venice and I was sold immediately! It has all the elements of a Venetian dish; strong in flavour and dark in colour. Many dishes have a little grubby-feel to them with lots of squid ink pasta, lagoon caught shrimps and anchovies. Bigoli is no different and is a classic Venetian dish. Imagine eating this and envisioning yourself at a little canal-side trattoria with a peach Bellini in hand.

**DF**

**Serves 2**

3 red onions and 1 banana shallot, all thinly sliced
(about 400g onions in total)
1 small garlic clove, diced
10 anchovy fillets in olive oil, roughly chopped
6 tbsp olive oil
1 tsp finely chopped parsley for garnish
180g spaghetti/bucatini pasta
Salt and pepper

Place a large saucepan on a medium to high heat and add the olive oil to warm followed by the sliced onions. Fry the onions for about 6 minutes mixing every so often until they start to reduce and caramelise. Then add the anchovies and cook for another 4 minutes using the back of a wooden spoon to break them up. Add in the diced garlic and fry for another 2 minutes. Bring a saucepan of salted water to a rolling boil and add the pasta to cook to al dente which is usually around 9-10 minutes.

Next, add about 160ml of the starchy cooking water to loosen the sauce. Add pepper and salt and taste to check the seasoning. The pasta should now be ready to drain and then toss through the sauce. Mix well so that the pasta is evenly coated. Serve straight away with a little extra olive oil and a sprinkle of chopped parsley.

# THAI CRAB, AVOCADO, NAM PLA PRIK

This is another sauce that epitomises the theme for this book. It's a Thai sauce that is usually served alongside plain dishes to spice them up. I love mixing it with crab and it makes a great one for a party!

**DF**

**Serves 2**

2 slices of toast
250g crab meat (mostly white but with a little brown is a good balance)
1 avocado, diced
½ a lime for serving
Cress for serving

**For the Nam Pla Prik sauce**
1 tbsp chopped coriander
1 tsp garlic, mashed into a paste
1 Thai chilli, finely chopped
1 tbsp ginger, grated and then chopped finely
Zest and juice of 1 lime
1 tsp fish sauce/vegetarian fish sauce
1 tsp caster sugar
1 tsp apple cider vinegar
Pepper

In a bowl, add all the ingredients together for the sauce and mix. It should have a rough consistency and have texture. Taste to check the seasoning, adding in more sugar or lime juice to balance out the flavours.

Prep the crab and avocado on top of the toast, with the cress and the sauce. Serve with the lime on the side!

This is another recipe that was created in lockdown. We had an abundance of spinach growing in the garden so we threw it into every soup, salad or stir-fry where possible. This idea actually comes from Peru where they use similar ingredients to a pesto but instead of basil, they use spinach and add cooked onions. This is a plant-based recipe but of course, add in whatever cheese you have. If keeping it vegan, then you could add in some nutritional yeast. Also, some fried asparagus would be nice tossed in at the end!!

**VEGAN | GF**

**Serves 2**

100g spinach
3 leaves of wild garlic (when in season)/3 garlic cloves, diced
120ml extra virgin olive oil
1 medium white onion, diced
60g almonds
30g basil including stalks
A pinch of caster sugar
Zest of a lemon and 2-3 tbsp juice
1 tsp white wine vinegar
50ml water
Salt and pepper

Fry the diced onion in 2 tablespoons of olive oil until softened. Add in the garlic cloves if using and cook for another minute. Remove from the heat and on to a plate. Leave to cool for a few minutes.

Blanch the spinach in boiling water for 30 seconds. Then run under cold water and squeeze the water out. Roughly chop up and add to a blender. Then add the cooked onions, garlic or wild garlic leaves if using, 2/3 almonds, basil, sugar, zest and lemon juice, vinegar, water, 50ml olive oil, salt and pepper. Blend to a smooth consistency and then add in the last almonds to break up just once. Scrape into a bowl stirring in the remainder of the olive oil. Check the seasoning at this point and then add to the pasta of your choice. You can add a little of the starchy pasta water to create more of a sauce. This keeps well for 3 days!

# SAUMON EN PAPILLOTE

This is simplicity at its best and I was first inspired by the chef, Shuko Oda at London's Koya who did a version of these flavours with tin foil. Here a paper parcel works better because it's more environmentally friendly than foil and the food won't get contaminated with any metal. Make sure you slice the veg finely so that it cooks quickly. Cooking temperatures do vary depending on the thickness of the fish.

**DF**

**Serves 1**

Handful enoki mushrooms (any other mushrooms will
do as long as they are sliced thinly)
⅓ carrot, peeled and then use a peeler to cut into thin strips
3 asparagus, ends trimmed and sliced into quarters lengthways
2 tbsp toasted sesame oil
1 fillet of salmon (120g)
1 tsp miso paste
1 tbsp cold water
A small bunch of coriander
Salt and pepper

**Quick ponzu**
1 tbsp tamari soya sauce
1 tbsp rice wine vinegar or white wine vinegar
2-3 tbsp lime juice and the zest of a whole lime

In a small bowl, mix the miso, water and sesame oil.

Prep a large piece of baking paper (about A3 or enough to encase the fish and veg). Add the fish fillet and the vegetables in the lower third section of the parchment paper. Season with pepper and a small pinch of salt. Carefully pour over the miso dressing and then fold the top half of the parchment over the fish to make a rectangle. Starting with one edge, tightly roll up the parchment paper until no liquid can escape. Repeat with the other two edges, then place the parcel on a baking sheet and bake for 15 minutes before having a look to see if the salmon is cooked. If still a little pink, then cook for another 1-2 minutes. Pour the package contents on to a plate and drizzle over the leftover juices.

While the fish is baking, in a small bowl mix together the ingredients for a simple ponzu dressing. Pour this over everything, add some coriander and a little more black pepper. Eat simply or with some rice or quick-cook noodles.

# ONE PAN PASTA

This is a bit of a twist on puttanesca and is a good one for when you are flying solo and very hungry. You can add whichever quick-cook veg you have but just make sure you slice them up thinly enough. If using spaghetti make sure that you use a large enough pan with a lid. Also, the pasta needs to be properly submerged under the water to cook.

**DF**

**Serves 1**

2 tbsp olive oil
180g cherry tomatoes, halved
1 large garlic clove, diced
A handful of basil
4 anchovies, diced
2 tbsp white wine
A handful of black olives
100g pasta of your choice
350ml freshly boiled water
80g broccoli, cut into small florets
A handful of green beans, halved
Zest of half a lemon and few drops of juice
Salt and pepper
Extra virgin olive oil for serving

Prep a large saucepan with a lid. Set a pan on a medium to high heat and add the olive oil. Then add the tomato halves and fry for 2 minutes. Finely chop the basil stalks and add this to the pan along with the garlic, anchovies, white wine and black olives. Fry for another minute to allow the alcohol to evaporate. Then turn down to a simmer and cover leaving a small gap for 3 minutes. Add the pasta and pour over the boiled water, turning the heat up. Season with salt, pepper and cover for 5 minutes. Then add the broccoli and beans and cook for another 6 minutes or until everything is cooked and the pasta is al dente. This is providing your spaghetti takes 10 minutes to cook. For other pastas, you might need to adjust the cooking times. Season with lemon zest, basil leaves and a drizzle of extra virgin olive oil.

# KOREAN JAPCHAE NOODLES WITH CRISPY TOFU

———

Japchae ("jap" meaning mix and "chae" meaning vegetable) is a classic Korean dish and often uses mushrooms and carrots. I cooked these for a video for Ella Mills from Deliciously Ella and she loved them.

**VEGAN | GF**

**Serves 2**

150g glass/cellophane noodles
2 tbsp sunflower oil
1 medium aubergine, cut
into chunks
½ red onion, thinly sliced
1 red pepper, thinly sliced lengthways
1 garlic clove, grated
150g white cabbage, thinly sliced
A handful of baby spinach
A handful of chopped cashews
1 tbsp sesame seeds
A handful of coriander,
roughly chopped
1 lime for garnishing, optional

**For the crispy tofu**
1 tbsp sunflower oil/coconut oil
120g firm tofu
A pinch of dried chilli flakes
Sea salt and black pepper

**For the sesame seed marinade**
4 tbsp soya sauce
4 tbsp toasted sesame oil
2 tbsp mirin wine
3 tbsp rice wine vinegar
1 tbsp maple syrup
1 tbsp grated ginger
(about a large thumb)
Zest and juice of 1 lime

Set a large non-stick frying pan on a medium to high heat and pour in the sunflower oil. Next, add in the chopped aubergine and fry everything for about 5 minutes until it has softened. Add in the pepper and red onion, frying for 2 minutes before grating in the garlic clove. Next, add in the chopped cabbage and leave to fry for 5 minutes or until everything has reduced in size. Season with salt, pepper and a squeeze of lime juice before removing from the heat.

Put all of the marinade ingredients into a bowl and mix together. Taste to check the seasoning.

Put the noodles into a bowl and cover in newly boiled water leaving for about 4 minutes. Drain and add to a large bowl. Pour over the sautéed veg from the pan, roughly chopped spinach, sesame marinade and toss everything together.

Using the same frying pan without washing, set on a medium to high heat and add one

tablespoon of oil. Using the larger grater side, grate the firm tofu straight into the pan. Season generously with salt, pepper and a pinch of chilli flakes. Fry for about 2 minutes or until they start to crisp up and colour. Serve with the noodles a handful of chopped nuts, coriander, sesame seeds.

# PRAWN SALAD WITH NUOC CHAM SAUCE

Traditionally a Vietnamese sauce to go with pork, fish or veggies. This is fresh and zingy! I first made this when I was out in the South of France and it is the perfect salad for hot weather. It has a wonderful crunch and the prawns are made to dip in the dressing. The fresh mint is key!

**GF**

**Serves 2**

500g raw medium-sized prawns, peeled with tails left on
2 tbsp sunflower oil
1 garlic, diced
1 lime
1 butter lettuce, torn into pieces
Large handful of coriander leaves
Large handful of mint leaves
150g bean sprouts
1 carrot, thinly sliced into sticks/batons and diced
½ a red pepper, thinly sliced into sticks/batons and diced
1 spring onion, thinly sliced

**For the Nuoc Cham sauce**
½ a medium carrot, diced into tiny cubes
½ mild red chilli, diced into tiny cubes
½ garlic, mashed into a paste, ¼ tsp
½ banana shallot, diced
3-4 tbsp white wine vinegar/rice vinegar
1½ tbsp honey
3 tbsp fish sauce
Zest and juice of 1 lime (about 3-4 tbsp)
Black pepper

In a medium bowl add all the ingredients together for the sauce and mix. Taste to check the seasoning, adding in more honey or lime if needed. Any leftover sauce can keep in the fridge for 3 days.

Set a large frying pan on a medium to high heat and add the oil. Then add the prawns and fry for 1 minute before turning over and seasoning with salt, pepper, diced garlic and the juice of half a lime. Fry for another 1½ minutes or until the prawns are pink and golden.

In a large bowl add in the salad ingredients, the prawns and pour over the sauce. Sprinkle the spring onions on top!

# VEG PASTA

I made this when I was doing veganuary and was craving a good pasta dish. You can swap veg to chopped cavolo nero, kale or chopped green beans. The pasta water is key here to make a nice sauce and you could add a splash of white wine just before you add the pasta water.

**VEGAN**

**Serves 2**

4 tbsp olive oil
1½ white onion, diced
1 celery stick, diced
1 medium carrot, diced
2 garlic cloves, diced
1 tsp tomato puree
Half a broccoli head sliced into small florets, dice the stalk

A handful of cherry tomatoes, roughly chopped
½ vegetable stock cube
150ml starchy pasta water
100g mushrooms, thinly sliced
100g baby spinach
A few drops lemon juice
Salt and pepper
200g pasta of your choice

Prep all the veg!

Set a large saucepan to boil and salt the water. Then set a large frying pan on a medium to high heat and add the olive oil. Next add the onions, celery, carrots and chopped broccoli stalks. Fry for about 5 minutes and season with salt and pepper. The veg should start to colour a little. Then add the garlic and fry for another minute before spooning in the tomato puree and mix.

Now the pasta water should be boiling, cook the pasta according to the packet's directions. Halfway through cooking, save a good 2 cups of the starchy water. Then drain when ready!

Back to the sauce! Add the chopped tomatoes, crumble in the veg stock, broccoli florets, chopped mushrooms and add the pasta water. Simmer for 5 minutes. Remove from the heat and add the spinach and lemon juice. Check the seasoning. Add the pasta to the sauce, adding more starchy water if needed to loosen. Done!

# KIMCHI FRIED RICE

I love the way you can make this delicious plate when you have leftover rice knocking about in the fridge. This is healthy comfort food!

**GF | DF**

**Serves 2**

2 tbsp toasted sesame oil (or use sunflower if you don't have it)
1 tbsp sunflower
1 banana shallot, diced
1 thumb-sized piece of ginger, diced
150g frozen edamame/soya beans
1 garlic clove, diced
200g cauliflower, roughly chopped into small pieces
3 heaped tbsp leftover cooked rice (I used short-grain brown rice)
4 tbsp kimchi, roughly chopped
150g asparagus, blanched for 4 minutes
150g broccoli, blanched for 4 minutes
1 spring onion, finely chopped

Half a sliced avocado, optional
A handful of freshly chopped coriander, optional
2 hard-boiled eggs, optional
(I boil mine for 6-7 minutes in boiling water and then run under the cold tap for 1 minute. This makes for a gooey middle and an easy peel)

**Extra sauce**
2 tbsp tamari soya sauce
2 tbsp toasted sesame oil
Zest and juice of a lime
2 pinches of sugar

Mix the ingredients for the sauce together in a small bowl and put to one side.

Place a large frying pan on a medium to high heat and add the toasted sesame oil to warm up, followed by the diced shallot, ginger and frozen edamame. Let this soften for about 3 minutes before adding in the diced garlic and fry for another minute before adding chopped cauliflower. Let this fry for about 2 minutes. Now mix in the cooked rice letting it crisp up a little in places for about 2 minutes. Next, stir in the chopped kimchi and let everything infuse for a minute before adding in the cooked greens and half the spring onion.

Prepare two serving plates and divide the contents, adding on top some fresh coriander, avocado, boiled eggs halves and the leftover spring onion. Drizzle over the side sauce and eat straight away! It will keep in the fridge nicely for 1-2 days.

# CARIBBEAN PRAWN CURRY

This makes for a perfect quick dinner and can be eaten in summer or winter with brown rice. I usually don't put too much chilli in but if you want more of an authentic Caribbean flavour then add the tiniest bit of chopped scotch bonnet to the onions. I used to make this for Stormzy on repeat and with good reason.

**GF | DF**

**Serves 2**

330g shelled raw king prawns
4-5 tsp mild curry powder
Zest of 2 limes and the juice of 1
1½ red onion, finely sliced
1 yellow pepper, thinly sliced
1 red pepper, thinly sliced
3 tbsp olive oil/coconut oil
4-5 garlic cloves, diced
A small bunch of thyme
400ml coconut milk
160ml coconut cream
Sea salt and black pepper
A handful of roughly chopped coriander
1 spring onion, finely chopped
A pinch of dried chilli flakes or scotch bonnet (optional)

Add the prawns, 2 tsp curry powder, salt, pepper and zest of one lime into a bowl and mix together. Place into the fridge to marinate.

Set a large frying pan on a medium to high heat and add the olive oil to warm. Then add the sliced onions and peppers to fry for about 8-10 minutes on a slightly lower heat. Pull off the thyme leaves and add to the pan. After about 10 minutes the peppers should have softened. You can add the diced garlic and fry for another 2 minutes, mixing everything around the pan. Next, pour in the coconut milk, cream and add another 2 tsp of curry powder bringing to a gentle boil. Season with salt, pepper and the juice of half a lime. Scrape in the raw prawns and stir everything around so that the prawns can be cooked in the sauce. This should only take about 2 minutes and make sure the sauce is gently simmering. You can fish out a prawn to check that they are cooked before adding the zest of another lime, chopped coriander, spring onion and the chilli flakes if using. Taste to double-check the seasoning. Serve straight away with some short grain brown rice.

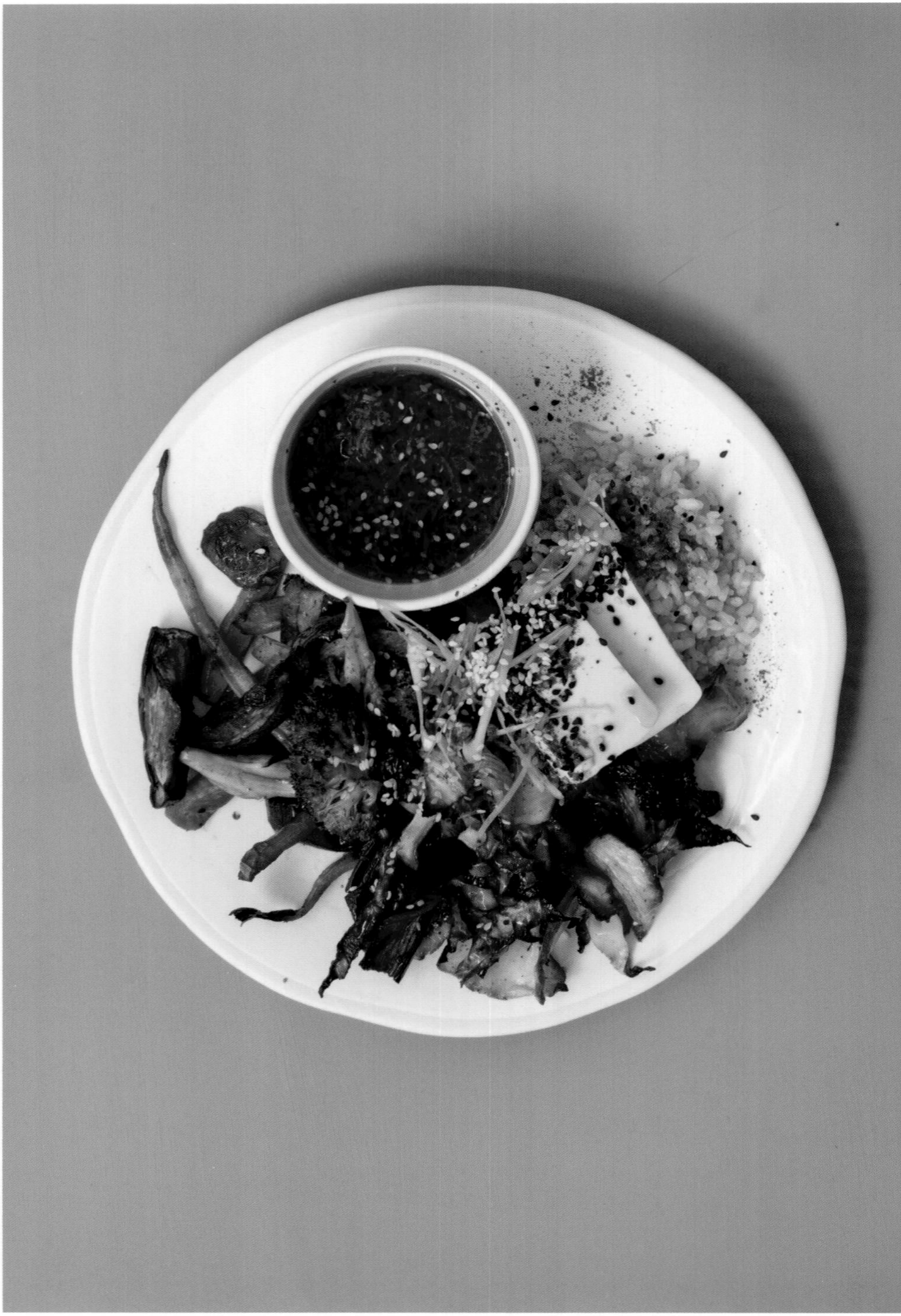

# JAPANESE INSPIRED FRIDGE FORAGE

---

I am in love with this 7-spice seasoning, shichimi. I first found out about it in a restaurant in Izu located 2 hours outside of Tokyo when it arrived with some udon noodles.

**VEGAN**

**Serves 2**

100g broccoli, cut into small florets
200g white cabbage, cut into thin chunks
½ an aubergine, diced
1 carrot, thinly sliced
70g shiitake mushrooms, sliced
Black sesame seeds
150g soft tofu
1 spring onion, thinly sliced

**For the marinade**
½ tsp shichimi seasoning
3 tbsp sesame seed oil
5 tbsp sunflower oil
3 tbsp soya sauce

**Extra dressing**
½ tsp shichimi seasoning
1 tbsp grated ginger
2 tbsp sesame seed oil
1 tbsp soya sauce
½ tsp maple syrup
Juice of half a lime and the
Zest of one lime
1 tbsp white wine vinegar

Preheat the oven to 190°C degrees and prepare a large baking tray. Add all the ingredients together for the marinade and lay the chopped vegetables out on the tray in individual groups. Drizzle the marinade all over and use your hands to make sure everything is well coated. Roast for 15 minutes or until the mushrooms and broccoli are done. The rest will take another 10-15 minutes depending on how thinly you sliced them. While the vegetables are roasting you can mix together all the ingredients for the dressing. You can also cook some noodles if using or just serve with some soft tofu.

Once everything is removed from the oven, divide the vegetables between two plates and add the tofu, spring onion and black sesame seeds on top and drizzle the extra dressing over!

# VEGAN BOLOGNESE

This should really be called The Incredible Mushroom Bolognese as it is pretty damn tasty. This is an awesome recipe as is has a huge depth of flavour and I think that it has the same satisfaction that you get from a traditional spag bol.

**VEGAN | GF**

**Serves 4 generously**

4 tbsp olive oil
650-700g mushrooms, roughly chopped into quarters for the blender
1 leek, thinly sliced
4 carrots, peeled and sliced into 1cm circles
2 red onions, peeled and chopped into sixths
5 sprigs of rosemary, leaves removed and roughly chopped
1 tsp dried oregano
3 tbsp tomato purée

14 garlic cloves, peeled
250ml red wine
1 medium courgette, roughly chopped into chunks
2 tins plum tomatoes (800g)
1 cube vegetable stock
1 tsp sugar
4 tbsp tamari soya sauce
2 bay leaves
A few of gratings of nutmeg
Sea salt and black pepper
320g pasta of your choice

Begin by pulse blending the mushrooms in batches. You want a fine consistency but not mushy. Put a large saucepan on a medium heat and add some of the blended mushrooms to the pan to dry-fry. Season them lightly with salt and pepper. Fry for about 2-3 minutes until the moisture has evaporated and scrape onto a plate. Continue frying until you have finished.

While you finish frying the mushrooms you can begin blending the rest of the ingredients. Add the red onion into the blender and pulse blend to cut into small pieces. Place these on a plate. Then do the same with the garlic, followed by the courgette.

Using the same pan, add the olive oil followed by the chopped leek, carrots, red onion, oregano and chopped rosemary. Mix everything together and fry for 4 minutes. Add in the tomato purée and stir for 1 minute before adding in the chopped garlic. Allow this to fry for another minute before pouring in the red wine. Cook for 2 minutes before adding in the chopped courgette, mushrooms, plum tomatoes, plus 1 tin full of water, veg stock cube (crumbled in), sugar, salt and pepper. Bring to the boil and then down to a simmer for 1 hour. Be sure to stir the sauce every so often. Then add the soya sauce and check the seasoning. Add more salt and pepper if needed, and simmer for another 12 minutes. Serve pasta al dente with the sauce stirred through.

# TOM YUM SOUP

My dentist, Dr Rhona Eskander, who is also my buddy, loves this soup and I so I set about making a plant-based version for her. Traditionally it is made with prawns so feel free to swap for a few if you fancy.

**VEGAN**

**Serves 2**

2 tbsp sunflower/coconut oil
Half a medium white onion, thinly sliced
3 garlic cloves, diced or grated
25g ginger, grated
½ a red chilli, seeds left in
(this will add a mild spice and you
can always add more at the end)
½ tbsp tomato purée
½ tsp unrefined sugar
3 kaffir or lime leaves (dried is fine)
1 lemongrass stick, outer layer trimmed
and bashed with a rolling pin and
sliced in two lengthways
750ml hot vegetable stock

160g Chinese broccoli (normal
cauliflower is fine too)
170g shiitake mushrooms,
roughly sliced
140g cherry tomatoes, halved
1 tsp mushroom powder
100ml coconut cream
1-2 tbsp Sriracha chilli sauce
Juice and zest of a 1 lime
1 tbsp soya sauce
150g silken tofu, cut into cubes
Small bunch of chopped
coriander, optional
Salt and pepper

I would recommend doing the chopping and vegetable prep before you start cooking so that everything goes smoothly.

Set a large saucepan on a medium to high heat and add a few tablespoons of oil. Add the onion and fry for about 3 minutes until it has softened and gone translucent. Then add the grated ginger, garlic and chopped chilli and fry for about 1-2 minutes. Next, the tomato purée, sugar, lime leaves, lemongrass stick and fry for about 2 minutes to release the flavours. Pour over the hot vegetable stock and bring everything to the boil and then down to a simmer for about 7 minutes. Then add the Chinese cauliflower and bring back to the boil and then simmer for about 3 minutes before adding in the mushrooms and cherry tomatoes. Simmer for another 3 minutes and pour in the coconut cream and mushroom powder. Remove from the heat and pour in the lime juice, soya sauce, Sriracha sauce, pinch of salt and silken tofu. Check the seasoning, adding in more mushroom powder, lime juice or chilli if desired. It should have quite a spicy, fresh but deep sweet and sour taste with a slight creaminess from the coconut. Try and fish out the lemongrass stick and lime leaves before serving or at least warn your guests. SO delicious with some basmati rice!

# LISBOA NOODLES WITH CRISPY TOFU

Taberna Rua da las Flores is located in the trendy Bairro Alto district in Lisbon and I feel that for me, it ticks every box. The interiors are cosy with pale pink marble tabletops, garlic hanging from the walls and a large blackboard menu that changes daily. The owner is a traveller chef and his food is a wonderful fusion of Asian flavours that complement the Portuguese seafood. Last time I was there, I had an udon noodle dish with crispy squid that blew my mind. You can, of course, add squid to this dish but I'm keeping it plant-based with crispy tofu.

**VEGAN**

**Serves 2**

200g udon noodles or any
of your choice
240g firm tofu, cut into 2cm cubes
2 pinches of dried chilli flakes
3 tbsp sunflower oil
Juice of half a lime
A small bunch of coriander leaves,
roughly chopped
4 pak choi, trimmed and
roughly chopped
2 tbsp toasted sesame oil

Salt and pepper
Extra lime for garnish

**For the marinade**
4 tbsp toasted sesame oil
6 tbsp sunflower oil
1 tsp ground paprika
2 tbsp grated garlic (about 2 cloves)
8 tbsp lime juice (about 1 lime)
2 pinches of dried chilli flakes
3 tbsp soya sauce (I use tamari)

In a small bowl, mix all the ingredients together for the marinade.

Cook the noodles according to the packet's instructions and drain.

In a large frying pan, add half the sunflower oil and half the tofu cubes. Fry, turning each one when a side is crispy. Season generously with salt, pepper and chilli flakes. This will take about 5 minutes and make sure about half the sides are golden. Transfer to a plate and fry the second batch in the same way. Then add the sesame oil to the pan and add the pak choi to fry for about 1 minute to soften before adding the tofu and noodles back into the pan. Squeeze over half a lime and the marinade. Toss everything together for 30 seconds and this should cook the garlic a little and soften the taste. Then mix in the coriander and serve straight away!

# PESTO PASTA

This is a dish that I tend to make quite a lot and it went down well when I filmed with Laura Fantacci and Petro Stofberg for their site Wardrobe Icons. It uses zingy fresh flavours, and depending on what you have in the fridge, I like to keep to green colours which I think makes it all the more appetising. Spinach and green beans are good or even some roasted kale. I have used brown rice pasta because it keeps the dish even lighter. It's perfect for the midweek meal or packed in your lunchbox!

**VEGAN | GF**

**Serves a greedy 2**

200g brown rice pasta
230g purple sprouting broccoli
150g frozen petits pois
100g cavolo nero
Juice of half a lemon

**For the almond pesto**
100g fresh basil, trim off just the very

ends of the stalks
100g almonds
170ml extra virgin olive oil
Zest of 2 lemons and the juice of half
A pinch of unrefined caster sugar
1 tbsp white wine vinegar
1 level tsp garlic, mashed into a paste
Sea salt and black pepper to taste

Take out a handful of the almonds and put to one side. Add all the remaining ingredients for the pesto into a blender and mix until smooth. Then add the remaining nuts and pulse blend twice just to break them up. Taste to check the seasoning, adding more lemon juice, salt or pepper if needed and place to one side. This will keep for 4 days in the fridge.

Put a full kettle on to boil. When ready add half the water to a large saucepan to boil and add salt. Trim the ends of the broccoli and when the water is bubbling add them to the pot for 3 minutes and then the frozen peas and cavolo nero for 1½ minutes. Drain the greens and fill up the same saucepan with the second half of the kettle water. Bring to the boil again and when bubbling add in the brown rice pasta. Cook according to the packet's instructions and drain when al dente. Run the hot water tap and wash over the pasta to remove the starch and tip the pasta into a serving bowl. Toss the pesto through the pasta, then add the greens and lemon juice. Che buono!

# BARSZCZ (BEET SOUP)

This is one for my Polski roots. My mum makes this sweet vinegary soup for Christmas and she uses the stock from the honey roast ham to give it some depth. Although that does sound good, this version is just as satisfying and veggie. I like to chop off the stalks and cook them in the sauce for later. They are so good and are often thrown away!

**VEGAN | GF**

**Serves 2**

3 medium beetroots including stalks (420g)
500ml hot vegetable stock
½ red onion, thinly sliced
1 tsp diced garlic/1 large clove
6 tbsp apple cider vinegar
⅔ tbsp caster sugar
Salt and pepper

Preheat the oven to 200°C degrees and trim the stalks off the beets to save for later. Wrap the beetroot tightly in tin foil and place into the oven for 45 minutes. Then unwrap and carefully peel off the skin. Thinly slice the beet and place it into a large saucepan along with the beet stalks, vegetable stock, onion and garlic. Bring to a boil and then down to a simmer for 17 minutes. Then stir in the vinegar and sugar. Season with salt and pepper and serve!

# LA LATINA NOODLES WITH TUNA & KIMCHI "MAYONNAISE"

I spent my year abroad in Madrid and I make an effort to keep coming back to this incredible city. Last time I was there, I visited my mates, Jack and Hugo, and they took me to this restaurant called Toga in the La Latina district. With industrial pared back walls and cosy seating, Toga serves modern Spanish sharing plates with some Asian flavours. They are most famous for a dish that isn't even on the menu, which is a red tuna noodle dish with a kimchi mayonnaise sauce. I completely fell for this dish!

**DF**

**Serves 2**

200g soba noodles
240g tuna fillets, cut into chunky pieces
3 tbsp toasted sesame oil
2 tbsp soya sauce (I use tamari)
½ a garlic clove, grated
2 tbsp sesame seeds
A small bunch of coriander,
roughly chopped
40g salted cashews, roughly chopped
200g blanched greens of your choice,
roughly chopped (broccoli spears,
green beans and mangetout are good)
Extra lime for serving

**For the "mayonnaise"
(makes about 200ml):**
70ml soya milk
100ml sunflower oil
2 tbsp white wine vinegar
Zest of a lime and 3 tbsp juice
140g kimchi
1 tbsp grated ginger
A pinch of chilli flakes
2 pinches of sugar
Salt and pepper

For the "mayonnaise", add the soya milk, sunflower oil, vinegar and lime juice into a fast-speed blender for about 30-40 seconds or until it has mixed into a mayonnaise consistency. Then add the ginger, kimchi, sugar and chilli and blend for a few more seconds until combined. Add to a bowl and season with salt and pepper.

Meanwhile, add the noodles to boiling water and cook according to the packet's instructions. If using soba, rinse under hot water after cooking to avoid them sticking together and drain.

Set a large frying pan on a medium to high heat and when hot add the sesame oil. Then add the tuna chunks and fry for about 20 seconds. Add the grated garlic, soya sauce and mix together for another 10 seconds before removing from the heat and onto a plate. You want the tuna to be seared but to still be pink. Plate up with the noodles, blanched greens, kimchi mayo and tuna on top! Sprinkle over with sesame seeds, coriander and a last squeeze of lime.

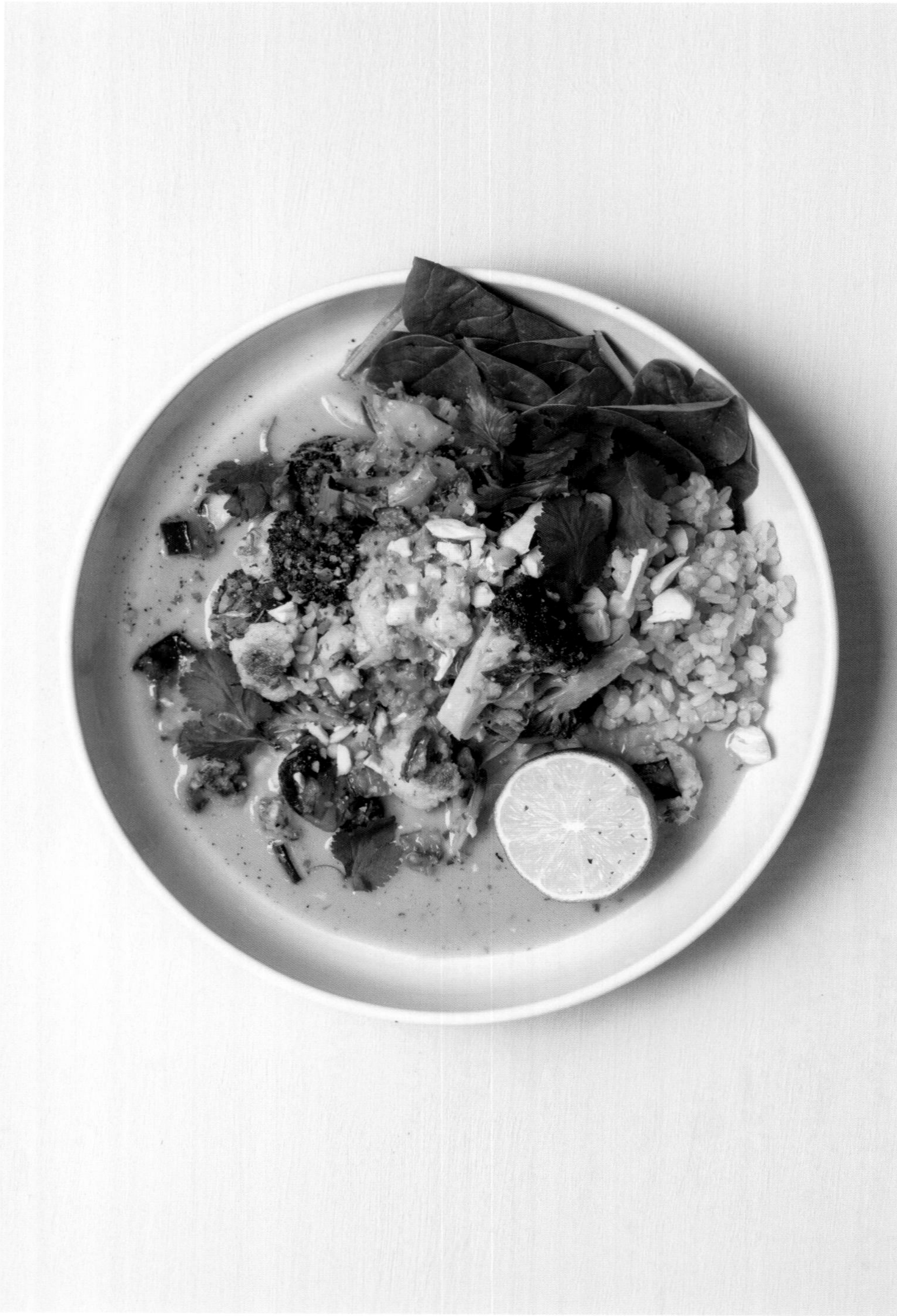

# THAI GREEN CURRY

This is a recipe that I turn to again and again. It is one of my ultimate TV dinners and it's also an excuse to pack in lots of veggies! A classic for a reason!

**VEGAN | GF**

**Serves 2**

300g broccoli, cut into small
pieces and thinly slice the broccoli stalks
300g cauliflower, cut into small pieces
1 aubergine, cut into small cubes
100g button mushrooms, big ones halved
½ tsp garlic powder
6 tbsp sunflower oil
Pinch dried chilli flakes or chilli powder
2 handfuls of baby spinach
400ml coconut milk
A handful of cashews, roughly chopped
Juice of 1 lime
400ml hot vegetable stock
Salt and pepper

**Curry paste**
½ onion/1 banana shallot
4 garlic cloves
1 large thumb ginger
1 lemongrass, the stem trimmed
and sliced in half
3 mild chillies or Thai chillies, (80g)
½ tsp coriander powder
½ tsp cumin powder

A large bunch of coriander
stalks (with the leaves saved
for mixing into the curry)

Preheat the oven to 190°C degrees and line two baking trays with grease-proof paper. Add the broccoli pieces, cauliflower, chopped aubergine and mushrooms to the trays keeping the vegetables in separate groups. Drizzle over 3 tablespoons of sunflower oil and season with garlic powder, salt and pepper. Toss the veg so that they are evenly coated and place into the preheated oven. The mushrooms can be removed after 5 minutes and scraped onto a plate. Then the rest of the vegetables should take 20 minutes. They will look golden and crispy but still with a little bite.

While the vegetables are cooking you can make the curry paste. Place all the paste ingredients into a blender and blend to a smooth-ish consistency. Set a large non-stick frying pan on a medium to high heat and add the remaining 3 tablespoons of sunflower oil. When hot, scrape in the paste and fry for about 3 minutes until the liquid has evaporated, it has reduced in size and darkened in colour. Then add in the coconut milk, hot vegetable stock and dried chilli flakes bringing to a gentle simmer for 1 minute. Carefully pour in the roast vegetables and cook for 1 minute before removing from the heat. Season with salt, pepper and lime juice. Serve in bowls with rice, the baby spinach, coriander leaves and cashews.

# ARTICHOKE PESTO

I seriously love artichokes although they are a bit of a bother to peel and sort out. My favourite way is usually by boiling them whole for 35 minutes depending on the size and then breaking off the leaves while dipping them into a lemon mayonnaise. This pesto is even more effortless to make! It's great spread on a quick toast or it's amazing tossed through pasta using some of the starchy pasta water to loosen and make a sauce. I had a similar pesto on canapés at my Spanish mate, Maria's wine tasting night and it was inspired! This uses few ingredients so try and find a nice quality jar of artichokes to max out the flavour.

**VEGETARIAN**

**Serves 2**

A few rosemary sprigs, separate the leaves
5 tbsp extra virgin olive oil
140g of jarred artichoke hearts in olive oil
80g parmesan cheese, grated
½ a large garlic clove, mashed into a paste
Zest of half a lemon and 1 tbsp juice
A few gratings of nutmeg
60g roasted cashews
Sea salt and black pepper

Set a large frying pan on a medium to high heat. Add a tablespoon of olive oil and swirl around the pan. Add the rosemary leaves and fry them for about a 1 minute to crisp up and then add to a blender along with the olive oil, artichokes, parmesan, garlic paste, lemon zest, nutmeg, half the cashews and lemon juice. Pulse blend for a few seconds. Then add the remaining cashews and blend for 3 seconds to just break them up. I like a cross between a smooth and rough texture. Scrape into a bowl and season with salt and pepper. This keeps well for about 3-4 days in the fridge.

# DAN DAN NOODLES

Originally a Sichuan street food dish with minced pork and a soupy noodle sauce, this is a far cry away from the original. In American Chinese food, the dish has evolved and they add peanut butter or sesame paste. I loved this idea and the simplicity of this recipe. This would also be great with pulled pork or chicken but it's pretty amazing as a vegan dish with any seasonal vegetables.

**VEGAN | GF**

**Serves 2**

200g soba noodles
200g green beans, roughly chopped
⅓ cucumber, peeled into ribbons
A bunch of coriander, chopped once
1 spring onion, thinly sliced
2 tbsp toasted sesame seeds
Sea salt and black pepper

**For the peanut sauce**
3 tbsp crunchy peanut butter
½ tsp mashed garlic
Zest of 2 limes and the juice of 3
2½ tbsp ginger, grated then chopped
3 tbsp Chinese rice vinegar
3 tbsp soya sauce

Set two large saucepans to boil and salt one of them. Add the green beans to the salted pan and blanch for 3-4 minutes before draining and running over with cold water. In the second pan, add the soba noodles and cook according to the packet's instructions. Drain and rinse in cold water to stop the noodles from sticking. Put to one side. In a small bowl add all the ingredients together for the sauce and whisk together. Taste to check the seasoning. Add cold water to loosen the sauce if desired. Toss together with the noodles, beans, cucumber ribbons and top with the coriander leaves, spring onion and sesame seeds.

# "CARBONARA" TWO WAYS

This is a "creamy" tasting pasta sauce without the heaviness of cream using soaked cashews.

**VEGAN | GF**

**Serves 2**

| Summer Greens | For the sauce |
|---|---|
| 200g brown rice pasta | 140g cashews, soaked in water |
| 150g peas, blanched for 1 minute | and then weigh out 200g |
| 1 courgette | 200ml almond/plant-based milk |
| 150g asparagus, ends trimmed and | 3 tbsp nutritional yeast |
| blanched for 4 minutes | A few gratings of nutmeg |
| 3-4 tbsp olive oil | ½ garlic clove, grated |
| | Sea salt and black pepper |

While the pasta is cooking, you can fry the courgette. Set a frying pan on a medium to high heat and add two tablespoons of olive oil. Use a mandolin to slice half the courgette straight into the pan and season with salt and pepper. After 2 minutes, flip everything around the pan so that all the pieces are cooked. After 2 minutes scrape onto a plate and finish the rest.

Next, drain the soaked cashews and place into a blender along with 100ml of the milk and the other ingredients for the sauce. Blend for about 2 minutes until you reach a smooth consistency. Then add the remaining milk and blend again. Taste to check the seasoning, adding in more salt, pepper or nutmeg if needed. Put the frying pan back onto a medium heat and add everything into the pan and toss together. You can loosen the sauce with a little more nut milk if needed as it tends to thicken quite quickly. Serve hot!

### Truffle Sauce
200g mushrooms, sliced and dry-fried in batches with salt and pepper

### For the sauce
Same recipe as the above plus 3-4 tbsp truffle oil, plus extra for garnish

Make the sauce in a similar way to the Summer Greens except with the truffle oil and assemble together with the mushrooms and pasta!

# SALMON FILLET, CHILLI SAMBAL NOODLES

There are a few sauces where the idea for this book was first born and this sambal is one of them. Throw this sambal into dressings, on eggs, rice and fish.

**GF | DF**

**Serves 1**

½ aubergine, chopped into 2cm chunks
2 tbsp sunflower oil, plus extra for serving
1 fillet of salmon
100g edamame beans, cooked
100g soba noodles
Salt and pepper
½ lime for serving

**For the chilli sambal**
**(makes around 350ml)**
200g medium-sized, mild chillies, tops trimmed and deseeded
12 garlic cloves, roughly chopped
14 anchovy fillets
2 medium banana shallots or
1½ medium onion, roughly chopped
10 tbsp sunflower oil, plus extra
1 tbsp unrefined caster sugar
1 tsp cumin powder
1 tbsp tamarind paste
1 tbsp fish sauce
Zest and juice of 2 limes

For the sambal, throw the chillies, garlic, anchovies and shallots into a blender and pulse blend until they are all roughly the same size. No more than a few pulses.

Set a large non-stick frying pan on a medium to high heat and add the sunflower oil. Scrape all the chilli mix into the pan and use a spatula to spread it evenly across the surface of the pan. Let this fry for about 7-8 minutes every so often moving everything around the pan. You might need to reduce the heat to avoid burning. Then add in the sugar and cumin powder and allow everything to fry for another 4-5 minutes. The sauce should have started to turn a much darker red. Once it's darkened and has reduced scrape everything into a small bowl and add the last ingredients. It should be sweet from the caramelised shallots but have a good kick.

Preheat the oven to 190°C degrees and line a baking tray with parchment paper. Add the aubergine and dress in a spoon of oil, salt and pepper. Bake for 25 minutes and then add the salmon to the tray and dress in the leftover oil and season. Roast everything for 10-12 minutes depending on the thickness of the salmon.

Cook the noodles to the packet's instructions, drain and run under hot water. Add the noodles to a bowl along with the edamame beans, salmon and aubergine. In a small bowl add 2 tsp of the sambal along with a splash of oil to loosen and toss through the noodles. Serve with lime on the side.

EXTRAS

Perhaps my favourite chapter! There are some amazing options here with spicy Asian inspiration and the ultimate bagna cauda with pickled vegetables. These can be paired with many of the dinner or party chapters, but you can also make a meal with them alone. The avocado ponzu is another winner!

# AVOCADO PONZU SALAD WITH CRISPY ONIONS

Perhaps the fanciest an avocado has ever looked!

**VEGAN | GF**

**Serves 2**

2 avocados, halved and pitted
A handful of sprouts
A handful of cashews, roughly chopped
A handful of coriander leaves

Crispy onions (you will have extra for salads/noodles):
150ml sunflower oil
2 shallots/1 medium white onion, finely sliced

**Ponzu sauce**
2 tbsp soya sauce
4 tbsp yuzu/6 tbsp ponzu
2 tbsp sesame oil
½ tbsp sesame seeds
½ tsp shichimi seasoning or chilli powder
A pinch of salt

Set a saucepan on a medium to high heat and add the sunflower oil. When hot, add one piece of onion to the pan. If it sizzles, then the oil is ready and you can add the rest of the onions. Fry until they just start to turn golden. This will take about 4-5 minutes depending on the heat temperature but keep an eye to avoid burning. Prep some kitchen towels on a plate and carefully drain the onions from the oil. Tip the onions onto the kitchen towel to cool completely.

In a small bowl, mix together the ingredients for the ponzu sauce and taste to check the seasoning.

Serve with the avocado halves on a plate. Drizzle over the sauce and top with sprouts, cashews, coriander and crispy onions.

# BAGNA CAUDA WITH PICKLED VEG

I think this is my favourite recipe in this chapter. It features some the best flavours; vinegar, anchovies, butter and garlic. I've had this in Italy and I had a memorable one on my birthday at Petersham Nurseries. Pickling the vegetables isn't classic but I promise this takes the format to new levels. I shocked myself at how good this was! A few things, the bagna cauda (warm bath) needs to be warm when serving and also the pickles. Trust me on this! Total heaven and the perfect nibbles at a dinner party. For a starter, I would add half of the recipe again.

**GF**

**Serves 4**

100g small rainbow carrots/medium carrots
cut into 1cm thick sticks
1 fennel bulb, sliced into thin wedges
200g cauliflower florets, including the leaves
500ml white wine vinegar
500ml water
100g sugar
1 tbsp peppercorns

**Bagna cauda**
4 garlic cloves
8 anchovies
50g unsalted butter
100ml olive oil

Set a large saucepan to a medium to high heat and add the vinegar, water, sugar and peppercorns. Allow the sugar to dissolve and come to a boil. Then add all the vegetables and cook for 4-5 minutes until it has softened but still has a little bite. Drain and add to a serving platter.

Add the ingredients for the bagna cauda into a blender and whizz until it is combined (roughly 40 seconds). Then add this to a saucepan and set to a medium to low heat. Stir every so often with a wooden spoon for 7 minutes. The sauce will look like it's curdling but that is how it should be. Pour into a dipping bowl and serve with the pickles.

# SEASONAL MORNING GLORY

This is one of my ultimate takeaway dishes. It can be tricky to find the vegetable morning glory so this is a version using easy-to-find greens with the sauce. Serve with noodles or rice!

**DF**

**Serves 2**

3 tbsp sunflower oil
1 garlic clove, diced
½ Thai chilli, thinly sliced
180g broccoli spears, sliced in half lengthways
200g spinach
A pinch of black sesame seeds

**Sauce**
1 tbsp soya sauce
1 tbsp brown miso paste
1 tbsp brown rice vinegar
1 tsp fish sauce
1 tsp oyster sauce
A pinch of sugar

In a small bowl, mix all the ingredients together for the sauce.

Set a large frying pan on a medium to high heat and add the sunflower oil. When hot, add in the broccoli spears and fry for about 2 minutes before adding in the chilli and garlic. Cook for 1 minute and then mix through the spinach for 30 seconds. Pour over the sauce, bringing the heat down to a simmer for about 1½ minutes. Remove from the heat and serve!

# MARINATED ENOKI ON AVOCADO TOAST

———

I'm obsessed with mushrooms in most of my recipes and enoki are my favourite! They are so delicious and also incredible fried in butter and garlic! If you cannot find them, then you can use a mix of button and chestnut mushrooms. It's really the sauce that brings it all together. These are great with noodles and I often use them as a side dish when creating an Asian-inspired menu (also pictured on pages 2&3).

**VEGAN**

**Serves 1**

140g enoki, ends trimmed
170g chestnut mushrooms, thinly sliced
1 medium avocado
1 large slice of toast
½ a lime
Salt and pepper

**For the teriyaki marinade**
13 tbsp soya sauce
1½ garlic cloves, grated
4 level tbsp sugar
4 tbsp chopped ginger
4 tbsp white wine vinegar

Add all the ingredients for the sauce into a small saucepan and bring to the boil for 2 minutes. Remove from the heat and transfer to a bowl.

Set a large saucepan to boil and, when bubbling, add the mushrooms to cook for 40 seconds or until soft. Drain and add to the sauce. You can serve straight away, but they taste even better when left to marinate for 20 minutes or longer.

In a bowl, mash avocado with a fork and add salt, pepper and a squeeze of lime. Prep the toast and spread over the avocado. Top with the mushrooms.

# CRISPY ONION | WINTER SALAD

This is one that I turn to again and again for dinner parties. Some burrata and roasted cherry tomatoes also work well. I highly recommend adding these onions to everything!

**VEGAN | GF**

**Serves 2**

1 red chicory/castlefranco
1 baby gem lettuce
¼ butter lettuce
Handful walnuts, roughly chopped
Handful sprouts

**For the crispy onions**
2 banana shallots/1 medium onion, thinly sliced with a mandoline
200ml sunflower oil

**For the dressing**
5 tbsp extra virgin olive oil
3 tbsp aged balsamic vinegar
Salt and black pepper

Set a large saucepan on a medium to high heat and add the sunflower oil. To check it's hot, add a small piece of onion and if it sizzles, then you can add the rest. Fry the onions for about 4 minutes until they start to go golden and crisp up. Be careful to keep an eye on them because once they turn, they can burn easily. Drain and place them on a paper towel to cool.

In a small bowl mix together all the ingredients for the dressing. Prep the salad leaves and drizzle over the dressing. Top with sprouts, nuts and crispy onions.

# MISO LEEKS

This is one of those recipes that sounds simple but the taste is anything but! It's this wonderful balance of salt vs sweet and it'll be the side that everyone remembers at your dinner!

**VEGAN**

**Serves 4**

2 leeks, slice in half lengthways and cut into 4cm pieces
40g caster sugar
2 tbsp sunflower oil
1 tbsp brown miso paste

Preheat the oven to 190°C degrees and line a baking tray with baking parchment.

Set a large frying pan to a medium to high heat and add the oil and sugar. Let this start to turn golden for 3 minutes depending on the temperature. Then lay the leeks cut side down into the pan and you can pack them in tightly. Roughly fry for 3 minutes and they should be nicely caramelised on one side. Carefully place each piece on the baking paper cut side up and spread a light layer of the miso on top of each piece. Roast in the oven for 10-12 minutes until a knife inserted goes in easily. You can prep these ahead of time and just warm them when needed.

# SPINACH OHITASHI

This is a simple, classic side that I had in Tokyo. If you can't get hold of kombu (dried seaweed) then you can use a very mild vegetable stock. I bought a batch back from Japan, and it lasts for ages and can be reused.

**VEGAN**

**Serves 2**

50ml dashi (kombu soaked in simmering
water for 30 minutes = dashi)
400g baby spinach
25ml soya sauce
1 tbsp mirin

Blanch the spinach in boiling water for 30 seconds and then rinse under cold water. Squeeze out excess water.

In a bowl, mix together the dashi, soya sauce and mirin. Prep the spinach in two balls on serving plates and pour over the sauce.

# ZA'ATAR ROASTED CARROTS | HUMMUS

I admit there are a lot of hummus recipes out there but mine is better!

**VEGAN | GF**

**Serves 4 and makes 350g hummus**

200g tinned chickpeas
3 tbsp extra virgin olive oil, plus extra for garnish
Zest of 2 lemons and 7 tbsp lemon juice
1 tbsp tahini paste
½ tsp sugar
2 tbsp white wine vinegar
2 tsp cumin
1 tsp garlic grated
2 tbsp iced water
Salt and pepper

**For the carrots**
600g carrots, 1cm sticks
2 tbsp olive oil
1 tbsp za'atar, plus extra for garnish

Preheat the oven to 190°C degrees and line a tray with baking parchment. Add the carrots and mix evenly with olive oil, za'atar, salt and pepper. Roast for 30 minutes giving everything a shake halfway through. Just before the carrots are ready, throw everything for the hummus into a blender, saving 50g of chickpeas. Blend until smooth. You can add a little more iced water if you need. I like to divide the hummus between two bowls with the extra chickpeas on top and roast carrots. Drizzle with a little more olive oil, black pepper and salt.

# SMACKED CUCUMBER

I've had this so many times and it makes for an excellent side for dinner.

**VEGAN | GF**

**Serves 2**

1 cucumber
1 tsp salt

**For the sauce**
1 garlic clove, mashed into a paste (1 tsp)
1 tsp caster sugar
2 tbsp rice vinegar
1 tbsp soya sauce
1 tbsp Sriracha sauce/hot sauce
1 tsp black/white sesame seeds
Salt and pepper

Divide the cucumber into 3 pieces. Use a rolling pin or the back of a knife to bash the pieces. Don't overbeat, you just want to crush it a bit. Add the cucumber to a bowl and sprinkle over the salt. Leave to sit for 20 minutes.

In a bowl, mix together the ingredients for the sauce. Pour this over the cucumber and serve with sesame seeds on top!

# CHILLI MISO
# SPROUTS | BROCCOLI

You can basically add this dressing to lots of cooked/steamed vegetables and it always makes it more exciting. Don't forget the fancy black sesame to make it look, well, fancy!

**VEGAN | GF**

**Serves 3/4**

150g brussels sprouts, trimmed and halved
1 broccoli, cut into florets
½ red chilli, finely sliced
1 tbsp black sesame seeds

**Dressing**
2½ tbsp white miso
3 tbsp sesame oil
8 tbsp water
1 tbsp maple syrup
Salt and pepper

Bring a large saucepan of water to the boil. Lightly salt the water and then add the sprouts for 1 minute and then the broccoli for 3 minutes. You want to blanch them so that they are soft but still hold some bite. Drain and mix together all the ingredients for the dressing. Toss half the dressing with the greens and plate them up. Pour over the remaining dressing, season with pepper, black sesame seeds and the chopped chilli.

A few one pan wonders and some of my classic dinner party sauces. This is a chapter about getting people together for a celebration. The few meat and fish recipes that feature in this book can be found here. We should all be consuming less meat and I wanted to encourage you to think of it as a special occasion. Then when the time presents itself, it should be enjoyed to the max. That being said, there is a vegan burger which will knock your socks off and could be given to any carnivore. Throw a taco party with some blue corn tostadas and try the vegan chorizo. This has been described as "meaty" and yet it is made completely from tofu and aubergine. I'm also quite proud of the crispy rice although it is the one dish that takes a little practice, it is beyond delicious and highly addictive.

# VEGAN BURGER, COMEBACK SAUCE

My cousin Andrew, who is a devout meat-eater and hardcore foodie, couldn't believe these were one: vegan and two: this delicious! These burgers are inspired by my last LA trip which pushed me to combine flavours and textures that I hadn't thought of before. I've named the sauce "Comeback" which is taken from the iconic Howlin'Rays chicken joint in downtown LA where they use a spicy mayo.

**VEGAN | GF**

**Makes 4 burgers**

140g cooked sweet potato
(about 1½ medium potatoes, baked for
50 mins at 190°C degrees)
140g soaked black beans (soak in cold
water for at least 4 hours or overnight)
Bunch of coriander
140g chickpeas, cooked
40g mushrooms, chopped
2 tsp mushroom powder
¼ tsp cayenne pepper
2 tsp garlic powder
2 tsp ground ginger
1 tsp onion powder
2 tsp miso paste
300ml sunflower
Salt and pepper

**For the comeback sauce**
4 tbsp vegan mayonnaise
(you can use the first 3 ingredients from
the La Latina "mayo" on page 122)
Zest of a lime and the juice of half
3 tbsp soya sauce
5 tsp gochujang paste (or substitute
with ½ tsp chilli powder/1 tsp chilli
paste to make 1 tsp gochujang)
1 tbsp apple cider vinegar
1 tbsp maple syrup
2 tbsp sesame seed oil
½ tsp garlic, grated
1 tbsp grated ginger

Weigh the soaked beans to 140g and add to a blender with all the burger ingredients except the sweet potato and oil. Mix to a rough paste. You will need to scrape down the sides of the blender and re-blend.

In a large mixing bowl, add the baked sweet potato and use a fork to break and whip it up. Add the blender contents to the sweet potato and combine so it is evenly mixed together. The sweet potato just acts as a binder so you don't want patches of orange anywhere. Divide into 4 equal patties and rest in the fridge for 30 minutes.

Set a large frying pan on a medium to high heat and add the sunflower oil. Depending on the size of the pan, you might need to add a little more oil. The oil needs to reach halfway

up the burger. Test the oil is hot enough by adding in a little flour. If it sizzles, then it is ready. Use a frying spatula to carefully lower the patties into the oil. Fry for 2½ minutes until golden and then carefully flip over and fry for another 2 minutes. Place on a kitchen towel for a minute before adding to the burger bun.

Add all of the ingredients together for the sauce and taste to double-check the seasoning.

Serve the burgers with toasted brioche buns, pickled onions, lettuce, sliced tomatoes and the sauce on top!

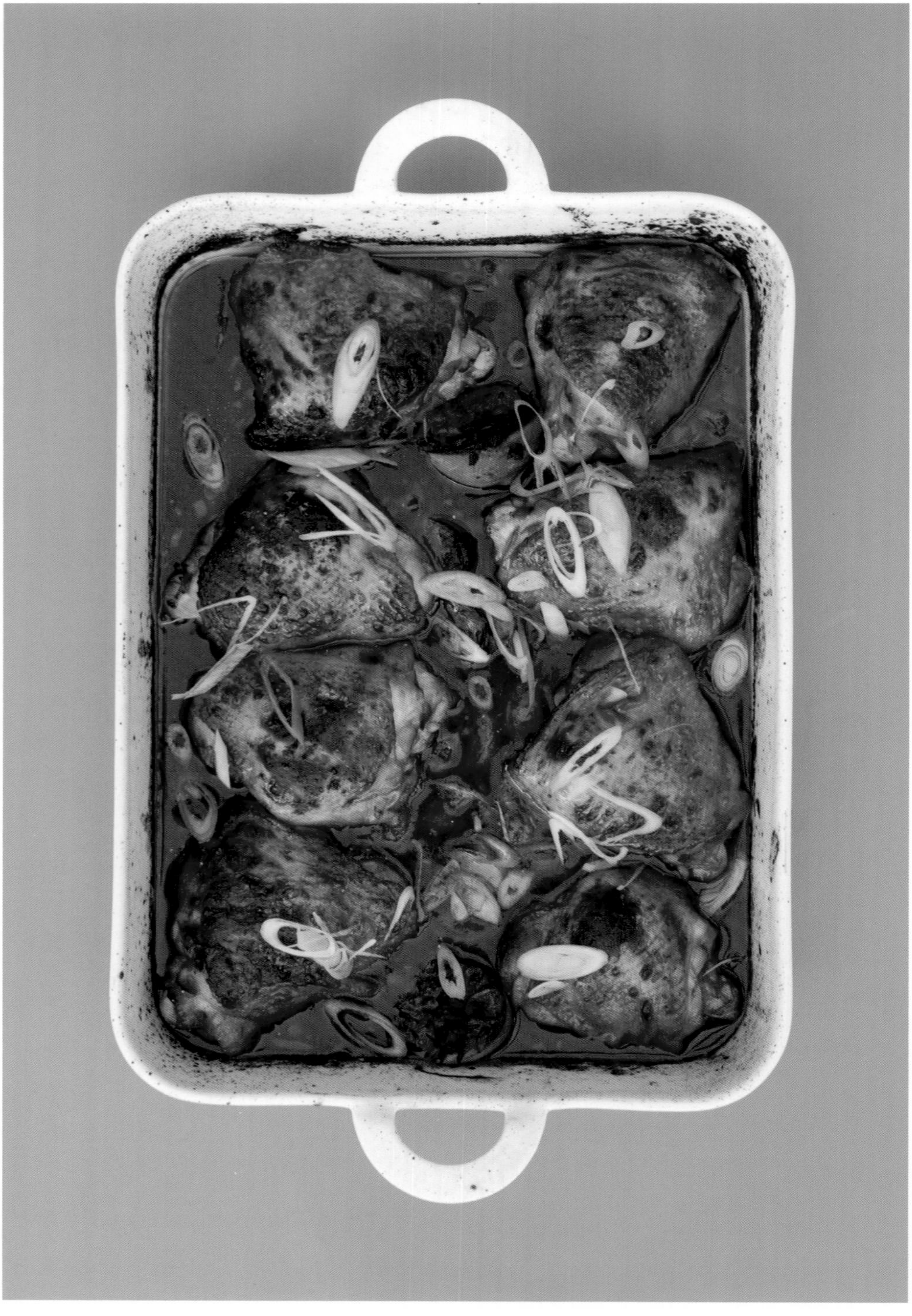

# GOCHUJANG CHICKEN

---

This is an easy traybake full of flavour and just needs some broccoli spears and rice to finish it off! I like to marinate the thighs in the sauce overnight which intensifies the taste. Adding in a tablespoon of gochujang paste is key for the Korean flavour but you could just add a few pinches of chilli flakes for a milder heat. This will make any dinner party!

**GF | DF**

**Serves 8**

8 chicken thighs
Spring onion, thinly sliced
Zest and juice of a lime

**For the marinade**
2 tbsp gochujang paste
6 tbsp toasted sesame oil
4 tbsp fish sauce
4 tbsp Chinese rice vinegar
2 tbsp sunflower oil
Zest of 2 limes and juice of 1 lime
10 tbsp honey
90g ginger, peeled and chopped
2 level tbsp ground ginger
12 garlic cloves, peeled, bashed but left whole
10 tbsp soya sauce (I used tamari)
Sea salt and black pepper

Place all the ingredients for the marinade together into a large bowl and mix together. Add in the chicken and mix together so that everything is evenly coated. Leave to marinate for at least 2 hours or even better, overnight.

Remove the chicken from the fridge to come to room temperature. Preheat the oven to 190°C degrees, and lay the chicken skin side down in a baking tray with the sauce poured over. Place into the middle of the oven for 40 minutes. Then remove them from the oven and turn to 220°C grill fan. Carefully turn the thighs skin side up and place back in the oven on the top shelf. Grill for 5 minutes to crisp up the skins. It might take longer but keep an eye so that they don't burn.

Serve straight away with chopped spring onion and the lime zest and juice!

# SPICED ROAST CAULIFLOWER, GREEN TAHINI

---

This is a real showstopper for a Sunday roast.

**Serves 4**

Whole cauliflower with leaves
50g pomegranate
1 tbsp sesame seeds
2 tbsp olive oil

**Marinade**
5 tbsp olive oil
½ tsp Aleppo chilli flakes (optional)
½ tsp paprika
½ tsp coriander powder
½ tsp garlic powder
Salt and pepper

**Green tahini**
4 tbsp tahini paste
Small bunch coriander (with stems, about 40g)
3 tbsp extra virgin olive oil
3 tbsp lemon juice
4 tbsp apple cider vinegar
1 tsp hot pepper sauce
½ tsp maple syrup
8 tbsp cold water

Preheat the oven to 190°C degrees and line a baking tray with baking sheet. In a bowl, mix everything for the marinade together. Remove the leaves from the cauliflower and slice off the stalk so that the cauliflower can stand upright. Place the cauliflower in the middle of the baking tray and use a pastry brush to start to cover in the marinade. Place the leaves in the baking tray and toss in 2 spoons of olive oil seasoning with salt and pepper. Cover the tray in tin foil and place in the middle of the oven for 1 hour. Then remove the leaves and tin foil and turn the heat to 200°C degrees. Drizzle over a little more olive oil on top to brown. Roast for another 30 minutes until it has crisped up.

While roasting, throw all the ingredients for the green tahini into a blender. Blend until smooth. Taste to check the seasoning and serve everything together with the pomegranate seeds and a sprinkle of sesame seeds.

# CRISPY RICE

This rice will be the star of any dinner table. I have added a goma sauce which can go on the side if serving with any veg.

**VEGAN | GF**

**Serves 4**

400g basmati rice
4 banana shallots /1½ medium onions, (sliced lengthways into 1.5cm pieces)
2 tbsp sunflower oil

**Rice marinade**
4 tbsp sesame oil
4 tbsp sunflower oil
3 tbsp soya sauce
½ tsp chilli powder
1 tsp garlic powder
½ tsp salt
Pepper

**Extra dressing**
3 tbsp sesame oil
2 soya sauce
A pinch of chilli powder
⅓ tsp garlic powder
A pinch of sugar

**Goma sauce (mix these all together in a bowl)**
4 tbsp vegan mayonnaise
2 tsp tahini paste
2 tsp white miso paste
4 tbsp toasted sesame oil
3 tbsp soya sauce (I used tamari)
2 tbsp rice wine vinegar
4 tbsp mirin/Shaoxing
2 good pinches of sugar
Zest of 2 limes and 2 tbsp lime juice
Pepper

Rinse the rice in a bowl of cold water and rub it together with your hands. You want to get rid of the starch. When the water goes cloudy, drain and cover with water again. Do this three times in total. Then pour the drained rice into a large saucepan and cover. Set to a high heat and bring to the boil and cook for about 6-7 minutes. The rice needs to have softened a little but still have a bite. Drain and rinse under cold water.

In two bowls, mix together all the ingredients for the marinade and the extra dressing.

Put the same large saucepan back on a medium to high heat and add the two tablespoons of sunflower oil to warm up. Then place the shallots pieces, cut side down, into the pan. Turn the heat to a simmer and pour the marinade over. Tip the rice into the pan and cover the shallots. Use a spoon to prod down the rice so that it fits in between the onions and touches the surface of the pan. Try to make the rice into a pyramid shape and then use

the end of a spoon to prod a few holes right down to the bottom of the pan. Then lay out a tea towel and place a saucepan lid on top. Fold the tea towel over the lid and place this on top of the saucepan. This will help steam the rice. Simmer on low for 17 minutes. Then check onions and see if they need a bit more colour. If they do, turn the heat on full whack for 2 minutes to caramelise more.

Now the rice on top should be perfectly cooked. Spoon this out into a bowl and use a spatula to scrape off the onions and crispy rice. Serve with extra dressing.

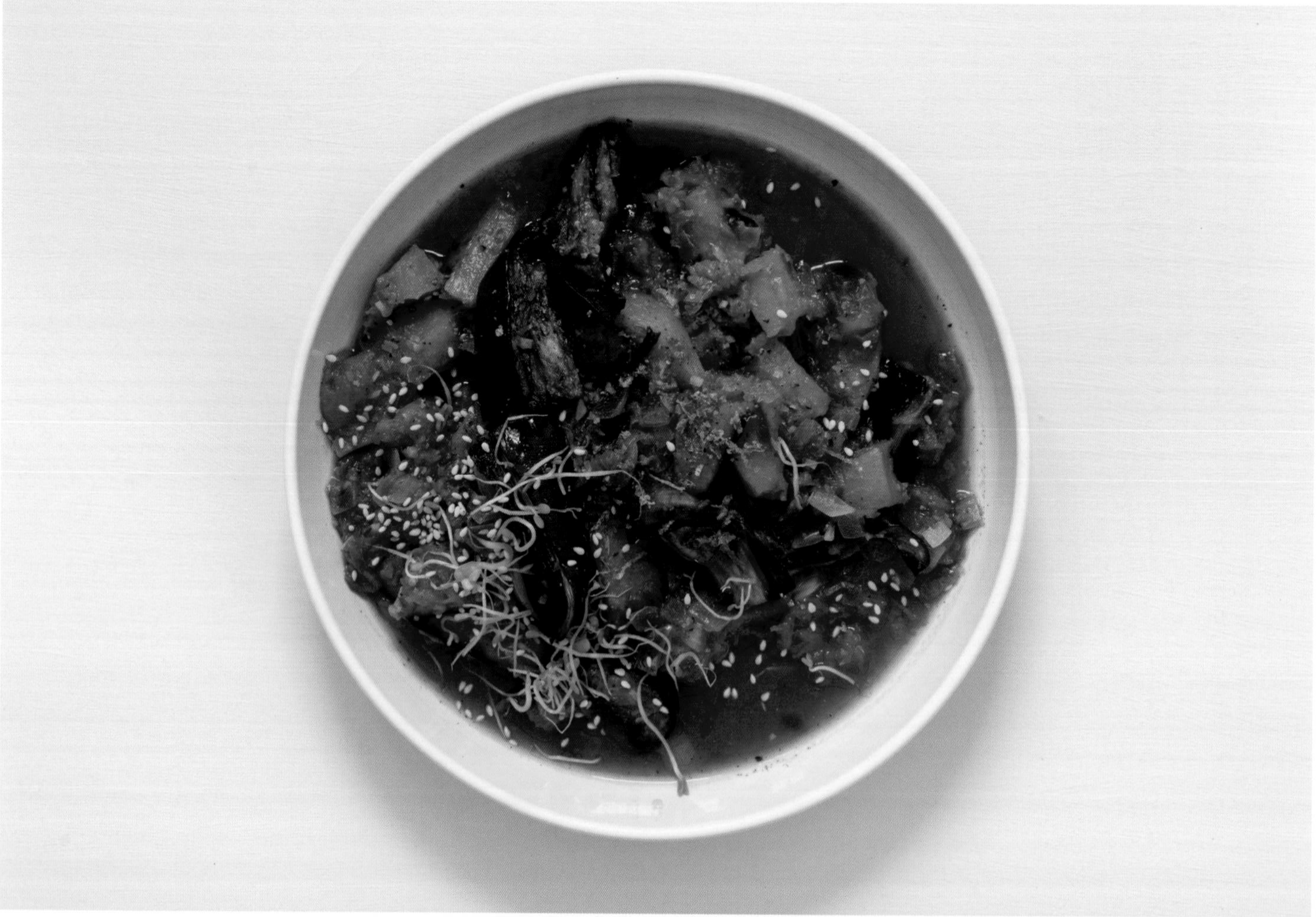

# RAINFOREST SQUASH CURRY

My neighbour and chef pal Alexandra Dudley and I hosted a charity dinner to raise money to help with the deforestation in Brazil. Everything was plant-based and the main was an onion squash curry with sesame, mirin and ginger that was executed by Alexandra. It came with a whole host of pickles, teriyaki enoki, toasted nuts, sprouts and some roast crown prince squash. I wanted to create a simplified version of this dish and this is a great contender. It uses the same flavours and throws in an aubergine. Feel free to add the garnishes to make it fancy for your dinner party guests. (You can use the marinated enoki from page 143).

**VEGAN | GF**

**Serves 2**

1 squash (1kg), deseeded, peeled and sliced into 2cm by 3cm pieces
1 medium aubergine, cut into long 2cm by 3cm pieces
4 tbsp sunflower oil
Salt and pepper

**For the curry sauce**
2 tbsp sunflower oil

1 red onion, diced
20g ginger, chopped
3 garlic cloves, diced
500ml hot vegetable stock
1 tbsp soya sauce
2 tbsp mirin
1 tbsp toasted sesame oil
1 tbsp brown rice vinegar
Zest of a lime and 3 tbsp lime juice

Preheat the oven to 190°C degrees and line a baking tray with baking parchment. Add the chopped squash and aubergine. Drizzle over sunflower oil and season with salt and pepper. Roast for 40 minutes until soft and golden. Keep an eye on it as the aubergine might take 5 minutes less time.

Set a large saucepan on a medium to high heat and add two tablespoons of sunflower oil. Then add the onion and fry for 3 minutes before adding in the chopped ginger and garlic. Fry this for another 2 minutes and then add in the vegetable stock. Bring this to the boil for 1 minute and then add in the roasted vegetables. Cook for another minute before removing from the heat and adding in the soya sauce, mirin, rice vinegar, sesame oil, lime zest and juice. Taste to check the seasoning in case it needs more salt and pepper. Serve with rice and coriander.

Le Club 55 is a place of good times, where you have a memorable meal, people watch and order a large panier des crudités with anchoïade. When I was last there, my mate Cammy ordered some grilled prawns and they arrived with a fiercely golden saffron sauce for dipping. I have kept my version very French, using cream and butter in the sauce. I would serve this with a butter lettuce chive salad with lots of lemon.

**GF**

**Serves 2**

**For the prawns**
650g/8 tiger prawns,
(shells removed for stock but
keep the heads and tails on)
1 lemon
1 tbsp butter
2 tbsp olive oil
2-3 tbsp white wine
2 garlic cloves, grated

**Prawn shell stock**
2 tbsp olive oil
40g unsalted butter
Prawn shells
140ml water

**For the saffron sauce**
3 tbsp olive oil
2 banana shallots, diced
3 garlic cloves, diced (about 1 tbsp)
3 pinches saffron threads
80ml white wine
100ml prawn stock
50ml double cream
½ tsp butter
A few drops lemon juice
Salt and pepper

Take the tip of a sharp knife and make an incision to expose the vein, which will either be down the back or running along the belly of the prawn. Set a pan on a medium to high heat and add a spoon of olive oil and 20g butter. Let this melt before adding in the prawn shells and fry for about a minute until the shells go pink. Turn down the heat to a gentle simmer and then add the water. Cook for 4 minutes to reduce the liquid a little. Then remove from the heat and leave it for 10 minutes for the flavours to infuse. Pass it through a sieve into a bowl and discard the shells.

In the same saucepan, set a medium to high heat and add 3 tablespoons of olive oil to heat. Then add the shallots and fry for 3 minutes to soften. Next, add the garlic and saffron and cook for 1 minute before pouring in the white wine. Allow the alcohol to cook off for another 1-2 minutes and then add the prawn stock, double cream, lemon juice and season with salt and pepper. Bring to a simmer and let all the flavours infuse. Reduce for a minute before turning off the heat. Stir in the butter and check the seasoning.

Set a large frying pan on a medium to high heat and add the butter and olive oil for the prawns. Lay the prawns in the pan and gently fry without moving for 2 minutes. Then turn them on the other side and turn down the heat a little, pouring over the wine, garlic, lemon juice and season. Cook for another 3 minutes. Plate up with the sauce on the side and pour the pan's juices over the prawns when serving.

# VEGAN CHORIZO TACOS

I'm not usually one for a meat substitute but this tastes far better than it sounds. I can't big this one up enough! Serve it with all the taco trimmings! This spicy marinade would be delicious with prawns or chicken too, but honestly try it with the tofu and aubergine. Total heaven!

**VEGAN | GF**

**Makes enough for 2**

200g firm Tofu, grated on the larger grater setting
100g aubergine, diced quite small (about ¼ of a medium aubergine)
4 tbsp sunflower oil
Salt and pepper

**For the "chorizo" marinade**
1 tsp onion powder
2 tsp dried oregano
1 tsp coriander powder
2 tsp paprika
1 tsp cumin powder
2 tsp garlic powder/3 garlic cloves, grated
½ tsp ground cloves
1 tsp sugar
½-1 tsp chipotle paste (depending on the strength of the paste)
5 tbsp sunflower oil

In a bowl add the ingredients for the chorizo seasoning and mix.

Set a large non-stick frying pan on a medium to high heat and add 2 tablespoons of sunflower oil. When hot, add the diced aubergine and fry for about 3 minutes until they have softened. You can squish them a bit with a wooden spoon. Then add the grated tofu and season with salt and pepper. Use a spatula to stop the tofu from sticking to the bottom of the pan and fry for about 8 minutes until the tofu starts to crisp up. Halfway through you can add the last 2 tablespoons of the sunflower oil. If using grated garlic, add it in at the 7-minute mark. Now, pour over the "chorizo" seasoning and mix everything together. Cook for another minute or so and then remove from the heat. Check the seasoning to see if it needs more salt.

Add this mix to the tacos with guacamole and an assortment of your choice. The following are good options: pickled onions, jalapeños, chilli oil, shaved radishes, crispy onions, coriander, chopped cherry tomatoes, fried cumin black beans, fried egg, soured cream, yoghurt and habanero salsa (pictured).

# ITALIAN LAMB, SALSA VERDE

---

I have made this for countless dinner parties over the years. It's pretty much fool-proof with maximum flavour. Keeping the bone in means that the meat doesn't dry out and you can have it ready hours before.

**DF**

**Serves 4**

2kg lamb shoulder, bone in
3 tbsp olive oil
12 garlic cloves, peeled
A bunch of thyme
A bunch of rosemary
1 tbsp dried oregano
Salt and pepper

**Gravy**
150ml red wine
200ml vegetable stock
1 tbsp apricot jam
Lamb cooking juices

**Salsa verde**
A bunch of flat-leaf parsley
A bunch of mint, discard the stalks
A small bunch of basil
3 tbsp capers
1 garlic clove, grated
9-10 anchovies
3 tbsp white wine vinegar
½ tsp caster sugar
Zest of 2½ lemons and the juice of 1
150ml extra virgin olive oil

Preheat the oven to 200°C degrees and prep 4 sheets of tin foil large enough to wrap around the lamb. Place the shoulder in the middle of one of the foil sheets. Season generously with salt, pepper and olive oil. Stuff the garlic and herbs under and on top of the lamb and wrap the tin foil to make a tight parcel. Do the same with the next layer making sure there are no gaps and then do the same with the last two. Place the lamb on a baking tray and into the centre of the oven for 20 minutes. Turn down the heat to 170°C and slow roast for 3½ hours. Take out the lamb and check that it is cooked through. It should be coming off the bone easily. Tip the cooking juices into a bowl along with the garlic and herbs. Tightly reseal the lamb and put to one side.

For the quick gravy, add the wine, apricot jam, stock and strain the cooking juice in. Bring to the boil and then down to a simmer for a few minutes until it has reduced and thickened. Season with salt and pepper.

While the lamb is roasting, throw everything for the salsa verde into a high speed blender saving 50ml of olive oil. Mix until it forms a smooth consistency. Scrape into a bowl and stir in the remaining oil. Taste to check the seasoning. You might need to loosen with a little more oil.

Just before serving, turn heat to 230°C degrees. When hot, uncover the lamb and roast for 8-10 minutes or until the skin has crisped up. Serve with the two sauces.

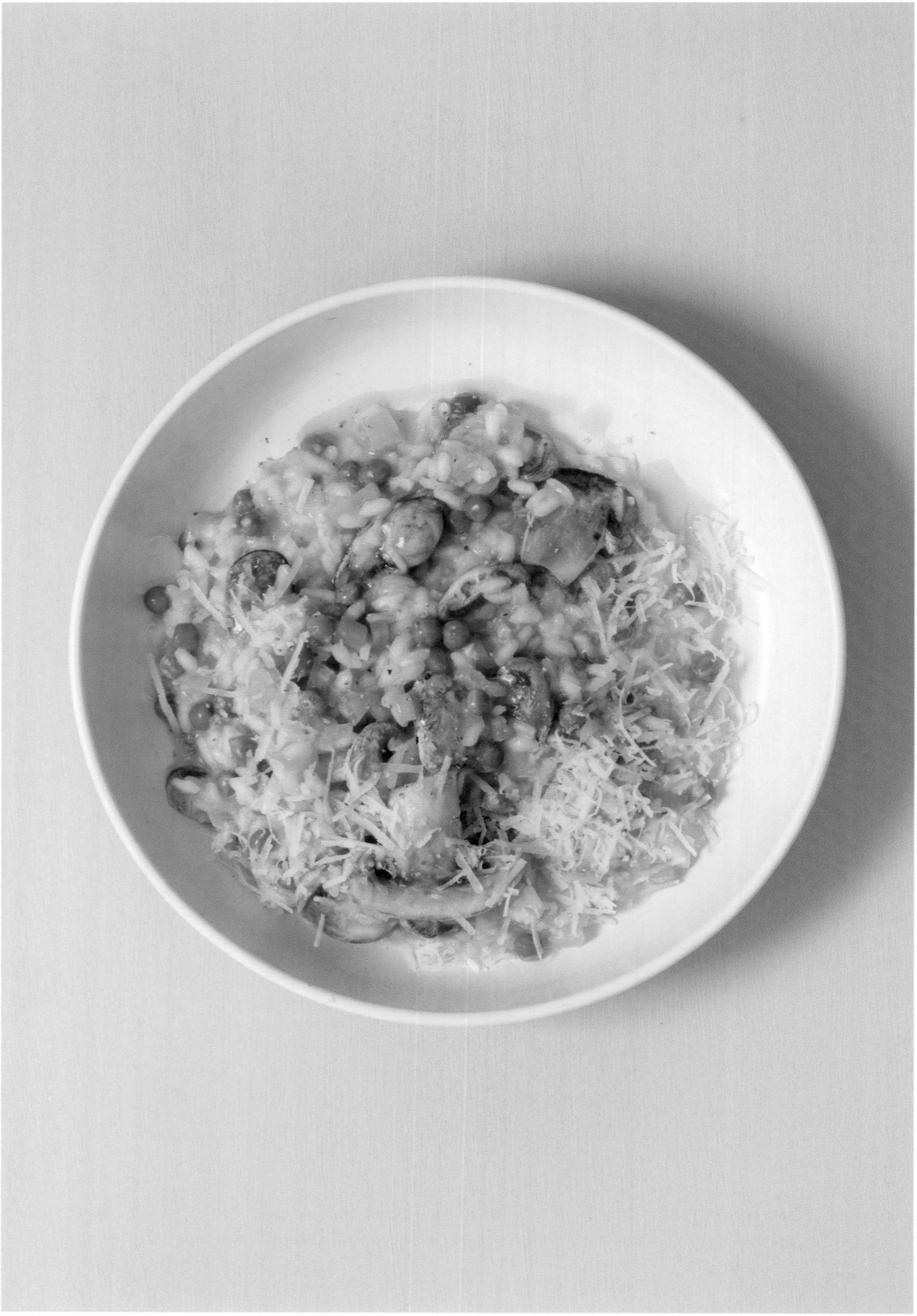

# IN SEASON
# VEGETABLE RISOTTO
# WITH TRUFFLE OIL

Another recipe that I perfected over lockdown and a great way to use up a homemade chicken stock from a Sunday roast. You can keep the base the same and then add in green beans or courgette for summer or roast squash for colder months. Having a good truffle oil can elevate a dish and just a few drops makes this humble risotto sophisticated. To keep this vegan, just leave out the cheese!

**GF**

**Serves 4**

2 tbsp olive oil
1 medium onion/2 banana shallots, diced
2 medium carrots, diced
2 celery sticks, diced
6 garlic cloves, diced
240g arborio rice
170ml white wine
1L hot vegetable stock
150g peas
200g mushrooms, sliced and dry fried in a frying pan
100g parmesan, grated (optional)
Zest of half a lemon and a few drops juice
4 tsp truffle oil
Salt and pepper

Set a large sauce pan to a medium to high heat and add the olive oil. Then add the diced onion, carrots, celery and mix for 4 minutes until they have softened. Then add in the garlic and stir for a minute before adding in the rice. Stir everything together and pour in the white wine and allow the rice to soak up all the liquid before pouring in a few tablespoons of the stock. Continue stirring the rice and adding in a little of the stock for about 17 minutes or so. You might not need all the stock. When the rice is soft but with a subtle bite it is ready, and taste to check the seasoning. Next, you can add in the peas, mushrooms, grated cheese, lemon zest and a squeeze of lemon juice. Season again with salt and pepper. Serve straight away with a last grating of parmesan and the truffle oil drizzled over.

# KUNG PAO CAULI

The combination of crispy verses sweet, salty and spicy is a complete winner. This is probably one of my favourite recipes in here. I love the way that you can turn the humble cauliflower into a seriously delicious dish.

**VEGAN**

**Serves 2**

1 whole cauliflower, divided into florets

**For the batter**
200g cornflour
100g breadcrumbs
½ tsp cayenne pepper
5 tbsp soya sauce
5 tbsp sunflower oil
Pepper
360ml water

**Sauce 1**
1½ tsp cornflour
7 tbsp soya sauce
5 tbsp rice vinegar

3 tsp mirin
3 level tsp caster sugar
180ml water

**Sauce 2**
6 tbsp sunflower oil
2 tsp dried chilli flakes
100g cashews
6 garlic cloves, diced
70g chopped ginger
Pinch of salt

1 spring onion, thinly sliced for garnish

Preheat the oven to 190°C degrees fan and line two trays with baking parchment.

For the batter, add everything into a bowl except the water. Slowly mix in the water. Dip a floret into the batter so that it is coated and place onto the baking tray. Continue until all the cauliflower pieces are on the trays. Bake for 25-30 minutes or until they have crisped up and cooked inside.

For sauce 1, add the cornflour first to a bowl and then add the other ingredients. Leave the water last to stir in to avoid any lumps!

Next, focus on sauce 2 and set a large frying pan on a medium to high heat. Add in the sunflower oil and the cashews and fry for 1 minute before adding in the rest of the ingredients. Let this fry together for 2 minutes. Now pour in the contents of the bowl for sauce 1 and simmer for 2 minutes. Let the sauce thicken a little before removing from the heat. Serve with the crispy cauliflower on a big platter with the spring onion on top and the sauce on the side for dipping.

# SEAFOOD TOSTADAS, CDMX SALSA

Finding a great fish tostada couldn't be easier in Mexico City. A standout choice is Contramar. It has a unique vibe with huge cobalt blue modern art, waiters in smart white suits and a terrace overlooking the bustling Roma Norte. La Docena had a tomato tostada that blew my mind and there was an award-winning option at Maximo Bistro. I love everything about this city and the tostadas are only half of it.

**GF | DF**

**Serves 2**

2 medium squid (140g), cleaned and cut into 2cm pieces
360g king prawns
4 tbsp sunflower oil
2 garlic cloves, diced
Juice of 1 lime
8 blue corn tacos
Salt and pepper

**Guacamole**
1½ large avocado
Juice of half a lime
1 tbsp olive oil

**For the CDMX Salsa**
4 tbsp apple cider vinegar
1 Thai chilli, thinly sliced, seeds discarded
1 garlic clove, diced
1 tsp hot sauce, optional
2 tbsp chopped pickled jalapeños
1 shallot, diced and rinsed under cold water for 1 minute
2 medium tomatoes
Zest and juice of 2 limes
1 tsp caster sugar
1 tbsp chopped coriander

Preheat the oven to 180°C degrees. Set a large frying pan on a medium to high heat and add 2 tacos to dry-fry for 2 minutes either side. Remove when they are toasted. Continue frying all of them. Add all the ingredients for the salsa into a bowl. Taste to check the seasoning, adding in salt and pepper to taste.

Add avocado to a bowl and mash with a fork. Add the lime, olive oil, salt and pepper to taste. Next, set the same large frying pan on a medium to high heat and add 2 tablespoons of oil. Add the sliced squid and fry for 1 minute until it starts to colour. Throw in one of the diced garlic cloves, season and squeeze over half the lime juice. Fry for another 30 seconds and add this to a plate. Add the rest of the oil to the pan and add the prawns. Fry for 1 minute on one side before turning over. Cook for another 1½ minutes.

Put the tostadas into the oven to warm for 1 minute. Plate up, turning over and season the same as the squid.

# COCONUT TURMERIC
# RICE BAKE

You get this beautifully golden-coloured rice from the turmeric and then the sweetness from the shallots dotted around. You could swap the squash for thinly sliced carrots or sweet potato. You just need to make sure that the vegetables are cut finely so that they cook through properly.

**VEGAN | GF**

**Serves 4**

200g basmati rice
5 garlic cloves, gently crushed so they stay intact
2 banana shallots/1½ medium white onion, finely sliced
100g baby corn, sliced lengthways
300g butternut squash, diced into small chunks
1 spring onion, thinly sliced
½-1 tsp dried chilli flakes, (optional)
2 level tsp cumin powder
2 level tsp turmeric powder
1 level tsp coriander powder
800ml coconut milk, hot with half a vegetable stock cube mixed in
1 tsp sea salt
Lots of black pepper
2 tbsp sunflower oil for greasing the baking tray

Preheat the oven to 200°C degrees and start heating up the coconut milk, stock cube together in a saucepan and add the cumin, turmeric, coriander powder and salt. Prep all of the other vegetables and grease a baking tray (I used a 20cm by 30cm dish) with a tablespoon of sunflower oil. Rinse the rice in cold running water for at least a minute which will stop the rice from sticking together. Then add the rice into the tray and spread it out. Place the corn, squash and onions on top of the rice and sprinkle over the chilli flakes. Pour over the spiced coconut milk and tuck the smashed garlic around the rice. There should be at least 1-2cm gap from the top of the dish to avoid any spillages. Carefully place into the oven and bake for about 40 minutes and the top should be golden with the rice perfectly cooked. If some of the vegetables need more cooking, bake for another 5 minutes. Scatter over spring onion. This is best eaten hot straight from the oven, but you can definitely eat two days after too!

# GRILLED TAHINI
# HONEY AUBERGINE

I first had something along these lines in a Greek restaurant called Suzi Tros in Notting Hill. They produce unfussy, good quality Greek food and this was by far my favourite plate. While making my own version, I thought that this would be a great dinner party dish because you can make everything else ahead of time and just grill the aubergine for 4 minutes when needed.

**GF | DF**

**Serves 4**

2 medium aubergines, sliced in half, flesh scored in criss-crosses
deep but without piercing the skin
1 tsp dried oregano
4 tbsp olive oil
1 tsp garlic powder/3 garlic cloves, diced
Half a lemon
Salt and pepper

**For the marinade**
4 heaped tbsp tahini paste
4 tbsp honey
4 tbsp olive oil
Pinch of salt

Preheat the oven to 190°C degrees and line a large baking tray with baking parchment. Prep the aubergine and then generously rub salt over the flesh. Leave for 10 minutes and then dab away the excess water. Place the halves into the tray and season with oregano, olive oil, garlic powder and pepper. Make sure you try and get into the cracks to spread the flavour. Bake for 40 minutes in the middle of the oven. Then turn them over to get rid of the excess liquid and brush the flesh again lightly with olive oil. Return to the oven for another 10 minutes and by then they should be cooked through. At this point, you can leave them until you are ready to serve.

In a bowl, mix all the ingredients together for the marinade. Spread this onto the aubergine flesh dividing between the four pieces. Turn oven to grill setting fan 220°C degrees and when hot, place the aubergine at the top of the oven for about 4 minutes or until the tops have gone golden brown and are bubbling. Squeeze over a little lemon juice and serve straight away.

CHICKEN BURGER WITH CHIPOTLE MAYO

# CHICKEN BURGER WITH CHIPOTLE MAYO

These work well for a big party as you can do lots of the prep beforehand. The burger itself is simple and you could add more spices if you like but the chipotle mayonnaise is what makes this really delicious.

### Makes 4 patties

1 medium onion, diced
1 tbsp sunflower oil
500g chicken breasts (4 fillets)
1 tbsp garlic powder
A pinch of sugar
2 tbsp chopped parsley
Zest of 1 lemon
1 medium egg, lightly beaten
2 tsp unsalted butter
Salt and pepper

**For the chipotle mayo**
1 medium egg yolk

150ml sunflower oil
Zest of half a lemon and the juice
6 tsp chipotle paste (depending on taste)
1 tbsp white wine vinegar
½ garlic clove, grated

**Extras**
3 tbsp chopped pickled jalapeños
4 tomato slices
4 lettuce leaves
A few pickled red onions
4 brioche buns

For the burgers, set a frying pan on a medium to high heat and add the sunflower oil. Then add the onion and fry for about 3 minutes until soft and translucent. Remove to cool. Next, add the fillets to a blender and mix until the flesh has broken down and is chopped. This should only take about 30 seconds. Add this to a bowl along with the garlic powder, onions, sugar, parsley, lemon zest and season with salt and pepper. Mix everything together and then add the beaten egg. Divide the mix into 4 patties and lay them out on a tray lined with baking parchment. Prod the centre of each patty once with your thumb to create a small dip and rest in the fridge for 30 minutes. Preheat the oven to 200°C degrees and add half a teaspoon of butter to the top of each patty. Roast for 15 minutes in the middle of the oven. They should be firm but still juicy.

For the mayo, add the egg yolk to a dry, clean bowl and use an electric whisk to mix. Slowly dribble in the oil and mix it in before adding a dribble more. Continue adding the oil in slowly until the mix turns white and thickens. Once half the oil has been added, spoon in the vinegar, lemon zest and juice. Then continue beating in the remainder of the oil. Stir in the chipotle paste, garlic clove and season with salt and pepper. Store in the fridge for up to 3 days!

# CHICKPEA MINESTRONE, FRESH TOMATO, CHERMOULA

---

You can make the soup base for a simple dinner or vamp it up for a vegan party with some grated tomato and this insanely tasty chermoula sauce.

**VEGAN | GF**

**Serves 4**

| | |
|---|---|
| 3 tbsp olive oil | **For the Chermoula** |
| 3 banana shallots/1½ medium white onions, diced | A bunch of coriander |
| 2 medium carrots, diced | A large handful of mint leaves |
| ½ red pepper, deseeded and diced | A handful of parsley leaves |
| 1 medium courgette, diced | ½ tsp ground paprika |
| 4 garlic cloves, diced | 1 tsp cumin powder |
| 3 tbsp white wine | ½ tsp coriander powder |
| 2 medium tomatoes, roughly chopped | ½ tsp diced garlic/1 small clove |
| 2 medium tomatoes, grated | 1½ tbsp tahini paste |
| 700ml hot vegetable stock | 100ml extra virgin olive oil |
| 450g cooked chickpeas | Zest of 1 lemon and 8 tbsp juice |
| 1 tsp cumin powder | ½ tsp Aleppo/normal chilli flakes, optional |
| 2 tbsp lemon juice | Salt and pepper |
| 2 large handfuls of basil leaves | |

Place all the ingredients for the sauce except the tahini into a blender and pulse until it forms a smooth consistency. Scrape the mixture into a bowl, stir in the tahini and taste for seasoning. Add in more oil or salt if needed.

Prep all the veg for the minestrone. Set a large saucepan on a medium to high heat and add two spoons of olive oil. Then add the onions, carrots and peppers, cooking for 4 minutes. Add the courgette, garlic, one spoon of olive oil and white wine. Fry this for 3 minutes and throw in the chopped tomatoes. Cook for 5 minutes and add the vegetable stock, chickpeas, cumin and season with salt and pepper. Bring to the boil and then down to a simmer for about 12 minutes, covered with a lid leaving a small gap. Add the lemon juice and stir in the basil leaves. Serve hot with the grated tomatoes and the sauce on top with a last drizzle of extra virgin olive oil.

# FISH PIBIL

This is a colour sensation! I love using any white fish here and you can even use this whole tray to fill tacos for a party. It's minimal effort but with maximum flavour. This dish can be swapped for chicken thighs if you prefer and you can marinate the chicken in the sauce for a few hours before cooking.

**GF | DF**

**Serves 4**

4 sea bass fillets
1 red pepper, deseeded and thinly sliced
1 yellow pepper, deseeded and thinly sliced
2 red onions, thinly sliced
4 tbsp pickled jalapeños, chopped
A small bunch of coriander and 1 lime for serving

**For the marinade**
4 tbsp olive oil
3 tbsp white wine vinegar
1 tsp cinnamon powder
1-2 tsp habanero chilli paste
6 anchovies, finely chopped
Zest and juice of 2 lime
Zest and juice of 2 oranges
10 garlic cloves, smashed, skins left on or 1 tbsp garlic powder
2 tsp cumin seeds
1 tbsp dried oregano
Sea salt and black pepper

Add all the ingredients for the marinade into a bowl and whisk together with a fork. Add 4 tablespoons of the marinade to a large bowl and set aside. Then prep a large baking dish and add the peppers and onions. Pour over the marinade and bake in a preheated 190C degree oven for 50 minutes. They should be almost cooked. Then add the sea bass fillets and pour the leftover marinade over. Season the fillets with salt and pepper and set to grill 220°C. Grill the fillets for 10 minutes until cooked. The fish is ready when it is gently flaking away. Serve straight away with all of those yummy juices along with chopped jalapeños, coriander and lime on top.

# ROCKY'S TAHINI TOMATO CHICKPEAS

Rocky is one of my best mates and this recipe is about weeknight dinners chez Rocky. We always have a chat about what we should cook, and I always end up saying "something healthy please." When Rocky likes a dish, she wants to make it every week and doesn't get bored with it. This is such a dish! Make this dish with a mate for when you are wanting a night in to simply catch up on some gossip on the sofa!

**VEGAN | GF**

**Serves 2**

1 aubergine, quartered and sliced into 2cm pieces
1½ tsp za'atar, plus extra for serving
4 tbsp olive oil, plus extra for serving
Few thyme sprigs
1½ tsp grated garlic (about 2 cloves)
490g cherry tomatoes, halved
100g chickpeas
1 tbsp tomato puree
½ veg stock cube
Few drops lemon juice
3 tbsp tahini paste, plus extra for serving
Handful basil leaves
2 handful baby spinach
50ml water
Salt and pepper
Rice for serving

Preheat the oven to 190°C degrees and line a baking tray with baking parchment. Add the aubergine pieces and coat in 2 tablespoons of olive oil, ½ teaspoon za'atar, salt and pepper. Roast for 15 minutes and then add another drizzle of oil before returning to the oven for another 5 minutes until soft and golden.

While the aubergine roasts, you can make the sauce. Add 2 tablespoons of olive oil to a large saucepan on a medium to high heat. Then add the garlic and thyme leaves and simmer for 1 minute before stirring in the tomato halves, chickpeas, tomato purée, leftover za'atar and stock cube. Season with salt and pepper and bring to the boil and then down to a simmer. Place a lid over the pan allowing a small gap and cook for 5 minutes. The tomatoes should have softened. Next mix in 40ml water, lemon juice and the tahini paste. Cook for another minute before tearing over some basil leaves and checking the seasoning again. Serve with the rice, spinach on the side, roast aubergine on top and a last pinch of za'atar and drizzle of olive oil and tahini.

# TACO TOUR MOJO PORK

---

It was hard to get around Mexico City without eating some meat, and pork was where it was at. If you're going to fall off the veggie bandwagon, do it on a taco tour! I tried a whole range of different tacos stuffed with slow cooked pork, crackling, fried onions, pickled onions, chilli salsas and guacamole. You could definitely use this recipe for a special taco night, and with this sauce, it brings it to new levels. I love the citrus blend in the sauce teamed with the jalapeños!

**DF | GF**

**Serves 6**

3 red onions, thinly sliced
2.5kg pork shoulder, bone in
3 whole garlic, cloves separated,
skins on, smashed
3 limes, halved
2 oranges, halved
1 tbsp cumin powder
1 tbsp coriander powder
2 tbsp dried oregano
8 tbsp olive oil
200ml white wine
2 tbsp apricot jam
100ml hot vegetable stock
Salt and pepper

**For the Mexican inspired mojo verde**
140g coriander, including stalks
50g flat-leaf parsley, including stalks
2 tsp cumin powder
1 tsp coriander powder
130g pickled jalapeños
140ml extra virgin olive oil
1½ tsp brown sugar
2 garlic cloves, diced
Zest of 2 limes & the juice of 1½
Zest of 1 grapefruit & the juice of ½
Zest of 1 orange & the juice of ½
2 tbsp apple cider vinegar

Preheat the oven to 200°C degrees and prep a baking tray large enough to hold the pork and two sheets of tin foil that will cover the tray.

Add the onions and garlic to the tray and sit the pork on top. Squeeze the lime and orange halves over everything and scatter around. Season pork with the spices, oregano, olive oil, salt and pepper. Cover tightly with tin foil leaving no gaps and place into the middle of the oven. Cook for 20 minutes and then reduce the temperature to 170°C and leave for 3½ hours.

Remove from the heat and the pork should be coming away from the bone but add back in for another 30 minutes if not. Place the pork on a plate and cover tightly with the tin foil to rest.

Turn the heat back to 200°C. Remove the lime and orange halves from the tray and add the white wine, jam and vegetable stock. Mix everything together and place back into the oven

for 8-10 minutes until it has reduced and thickened. Now turn the temperature to 230°C and when heated, add the pork back into the oven to crisp up the skin for 7-10 minutes.

Place all of the salsa ingredients into a blender. Blend until smooth and taste to check the seasoning. Serve pork with the two sauces.

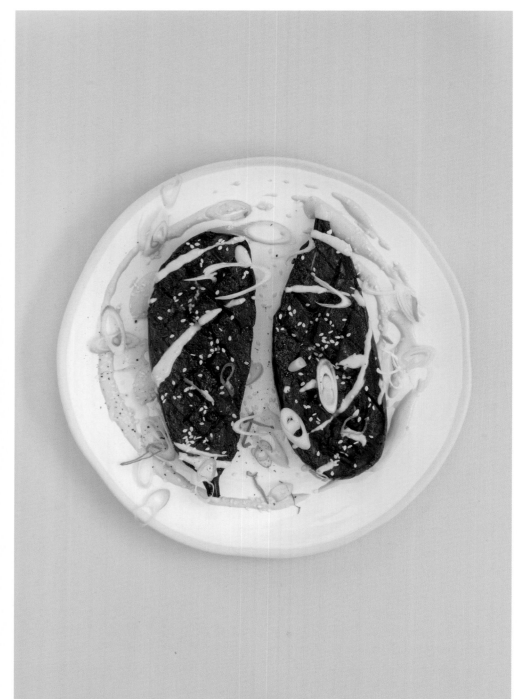

# MISO AUBERGINE

This is one of my signature dinner dishes because you can make it ahead and just warm when needed. It's actually pretty good as it is but the tahini cuts through the sweet and salty adding more depth.

**VEGETARIAN | DF**

**Serves 2**

1 large aubergine, halved
½ tsp sesame seeds
1 spring onion, thinly sliced

**For the miso sauce**
1 tbsp sunflower oil
1½ tbsp dark miso paste
1½ tbsp runny honey
1 tbsp toasted sesame oil
5 tbsp hot water

**For the tahini sauce**
2 tbsp tahini paste
Zest and juice of half a lemon
2 tbsp soya sauce
3 tbsp Chinese rice vinegar
½ tsp honey
5 tbsp cold water
A pinch of sea salt and black pepper

Score the aubergine flesh with a criss-cross without piercing the skin and place into a baking tray lined with baking parchment. Mix all the ingredients together for the miso sauce except the sunflower oil and spoon about ½ the sauce over the aubergine halves making sure it goes into all the gaps. Leave to marinate for 25 minutes, cut side up. Then cover the tray top with tin foil and bake in a preheated 190°C degree oven for 20 minutes. Remove from the oven and uncover the tray. Mix any remaining sauce with the sunflower oil and spoon over the tops again. Return to the middle of the oven for 20-30 minutes or until the flesh is very tender, almost collapsing and the tops are caramelised. While the aubergine is roasting you can start on the tahini sauce. Mix all the ingredients together in a small bowl and use a few tablespoons of cold water to loosen the tahini to a good dripping consistency. Serve miso aubergine with short grain brown rice, spring onions, sesame seeds and the tahini drizzled on top!

# LOCKDOWN CHICKEN

I spent lockdown in the Cotswolds with my sister's family (not too shabby). Every Sunday my brother-in-law, Josh, would make this chicken. He would get a good quality organic chicken and serve it with roast potatoes and puréed carrots. This onion gravy is pure genius!

**GF**

**Serves 4**

4 tbsp olive oil
1.7kg whole chicken, at room temperature
Bunch of rosemary
Bunch of thyme
4 white/red onions, thinly sliced
2 lemons, halved
1 whole garlic, broken up but skins left on
130ml red wine
1 large tbsp apricot jam
1 tbsp Dijon mustard
1 tsp unsalted butter
Salt and pepper

Preheat the oven to 190°C degrees and prep a large baking tray.

Add the chicken into the tray along with the sliced onions and garlic cloves. Stuff the bird's cavity with thyme, rosemary and lemon. Season generously with salt and pepper then drizzle over the olive oil. Turn the chicken breast-side down and place into the middle of the preheated oven for 50 minutes.

Then remove from the oven and carefully turn the chicken breast-side up. Mix the onions around the pan and add a little more olive oil if necessary. Roast for another 15-20 minutes or until the top is golden and the leg feels like it could pull away easily. Next, carefully place the chicken on a large warm serving platter and cover tightly in tin foil to rest.

For the onion gravy, add red wine, apricot jam and mustard to the baking tray and mix everything around. Place back into the middle of the oven for 12-15 minutes until the alcohol has evaporated and the mixture has reduced. Spoon this mixture into a blender along with a teaspoon of butter and blend until smooth. Serve straight away with the chicken!

If serving with roast potatoes, place on a tray in the oven for 45 minutes while the chicken is cooking.

# AUBERGINE À LA TOMATE

This dish takes me to the South of France and then to an amazing banquet that I prepared for Russell Brand and his wife, Laura. I had to make some flavourful vegan dishes and this was probably one of the most popular. This is a simplified version and is best eaten in the summer months with rice, greens and a large salad.

**VEGAN**

**Serves 4**

2 medium aubergines, sliced
lengthways into 1cm pieces
½ tsp garlic powder
1 tbsp dried oregano
5 tbsp olive oil
A few rosemary sprigs
Salt and pepper

**For the tomato sauce**
3 tbsp olive oil
3 banana shallots, diced
4 garlic cloves, diced

1½ tsp dried oregano
450g cherry tomatoes, halved
300ml tinned tomatoes
40ml red wine
½ veg stock cube
80g sun-dried tomatoes,
roughly chopped
1½ tsp balsamic vinegar
Bunch of fresh basil, leaves
and stalks separated
6 tbsp breadcrumbs for
topping

Preheat the oven to 190°C degrees. Lay out some paper towels and place the aubergine slices on top in rows. Sprinkle over with salt and leave to sit for 10 minutes. Dab away excess water and salt. Then divide between two baking trays and season with three tablespoons of olive oil, oregano, garlic powder and pepper. Bake for about 16 minutes and then add the rosemary leaves and the two leftover spoons of olive oil. Roast for another 5 minutes until lightly golden and soft.

While the aubergine cooks set a large saucepan on a medium to high heat and add 3 spoons of olive oil. Then add the shallots and finely chop the basil stalks throwing them in. Fry for 5 minutes before adding in garlic, oregano and the rosemary leaves. Cook for 2 minutes and then add the cherry tomatoes, tinned tomatoes (including half a tin of water) followed by the wine, stock cube, sun-dried tomatoes and season. Let it fry for 1 minute before bringing down to a simmer for 12 minutes, covered with a lid leaving a small gap. Then stir in the balsamic and two-thirds of the basil leaves. Check the seasoning once more.

Turn the oven to the grill fan setting at 220°C degrees. Grease a 20cm by 30cm baking dish and spoon in some of the tomato sauce to create a very thin layer. Top with half the

aubergine in layers and then top again with the leftover sauce. Arrange the second layer of aubergine and drizzle over with the last bit of olive oil. Place under the grill for 8 minutes and then sprinkle over the breadcrumbs and grill for another 8-10 minutes or until crispy. Serve with the leftover basil leaves. This keeps well for 3 days.

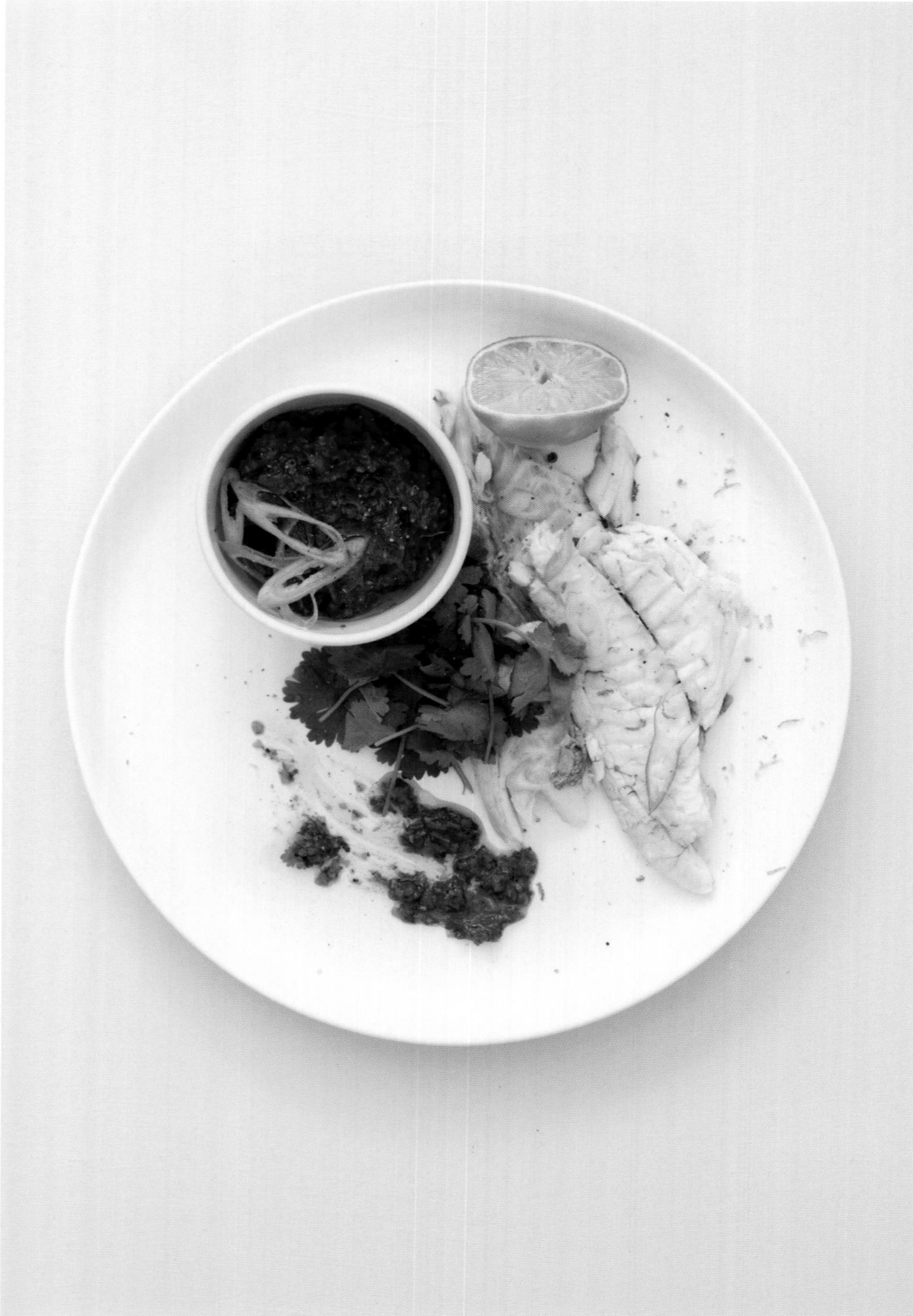

# TIGER BITE FISH

I first had this Thai sauce in a takeaway from one of my niece's school teachers turned caterer, Miss Mimi. She served it with chicken and noodles and the sauce did the talking. This is a really easy dinner to prepare for a small crowd as you prep the sauce before and a whole roast fish is far more forgiving than a roast fillet. You could slather it over breakfast eggs or even spread it on an open baguette with more chilli like my brother, Christian. This sauce recipe makes enough for an extra meal or two.

## Serves 4

2 whole sea bream
1 lime, sliced
Small bunch of coriander
3 tbsp toasted sesame oil
Salt and pepper

### For the tiger bite sauce
400g cherry tomatoes, halved
7 tbsp vegetable oil/neutral oil
1 Thai chilli

6 shallots, thinly sliced
4 garlic cloves, chopped
3 anchovy fillets, chopped
2 tbsp oyster sauce
3 tbsp fish sauce
Zest and juice of 2 limes
1 tbsp white wine vinegar
20g bunch of coriander
including the stalks

Preheat the oven to 220°C degrees on the grill setting. Line a baking tray with baking parchment and add the cherry tomato halves. Drizzle over two spoons of vegetable oil, salt and pepper and put under the grill for 10-12 minutes. Then add the chilli and grill for another 5 minutes. They should have roasted and charred a bit. Remove from the oven and add tomatoes to a blender including half of the chilli. While the tomatoes are cooking, you can finish the sauce. Set a frying pan to a medium to high heat and add three tablespoons of oil. Then add the shallots and turn the heat down to fry for ten minutes. Then add another two spoons of oil, the garlic and anchovies and allow the fish to melt into the oil. This will take two minutes. Scrape into the blender and add the fish, oyster sauce, lime zest, juice, vinegar and coriander. Blend to a smooth consistency and taste to check how spicy. Blend in the other chilli half if needed and then scrape into a bowl. Taste to check the seasoning add in salt and pepper if needed.

When the tomatoes are done, set oven to 200°C degrees fan. Using the same baking tray and paper add in the bream. Fill the fish's cavity with lime and coriander. Drizzle over with sesame oil, salt and pepper and place into the preheated oven for 40 minutes or until the skin has just started to blister. Fillet fish and serve a generous helping of tiger bite sauce on the side with extra lime, green salad and roast potatoes.

Anyone who knows me will know that I have an extremely sweet tooth. Desserts are where my career in food started and I find baking cakes and making ice cream meditative. Here desserts are enhanced with salted caramel, whipped coconut cream, spiced sugar syrup and blackberry compote. But if I'm honest, the frangipane sheet cake with whipped ricotta is great on its own. There are two chocolate birthday cake options; a classic sponge with buttercream icing and a plant-based version. The raspberry sorbet is unbelievably easy to make and the brown butter blondies deserve a book all to themselves.

# FRANGIPANE SHEET CAKE WITH FRUIT COMPOTE, WHIPPED RICOTTA

The idea for this cake came about when I went to an amazing place called Sqirl in Silverlake, Los Angeles. Their restaurant inspired in many ways, and they are known for an iconic whipped ricotta, jam brioche toast. I have displayed the icing and jam the Sqirl way here, although it does mean some people might get more fruit compote than others so feel free to spread it out evenly. Use berries for summer, rhubarb for spring and cinnamon, apple and pear for autumn.

**SPELT**

**Serves 8**

| For the sponge | For the compote |
|---|---|
| 200g unsalted butter, at room temperature and cut into cubes | 250g blackberries |
| 200g caster sugar | 1 tbsp caster sugar |
| 4 medium eggs, lightly beaten together | 4 tbsp lemon juice |
| 250g ground almonds | |
| 2 tbsp spelt/gluten-free/plain flour | **For the ricotta** |
| A pinch of salt | 250g ricotta, drained of any excess water |
| Zest of half a lemon | 150ml whipping cream |
| ½ tsp almond extract | 1 tsp vanilla extract |
| | 4 tbsp icing sugar |

Preheat the oven to 170°C degrees. Line and grease a 20cm / 8-inch square baking tin with baking parchment. Add the soft butter and sugar to an electric mixer and beat for about 5 minutes until light and fluffy. In a separate bowl, mix together the almonds, flour and salt. Then slowly beat in a little of the beaten eggs followed by a few spoonfuls of the dry ingredients. Continue adding in a little at a time of each until everything is incorporated. Lastly, mix in the almond extract and lemon zest. Scrape the batter into the prepared baking tin and into the preheated oven for 40 minutes or until a skewer inserted comes out nearly clean. Leave to cool completely before icing.

For the compote, add all ingredients to a saucepan and set to a medium heat. Simmer and mix for 10 minutes until soft and then remove from the heat and cool. Throw all the ingredients for the icing into a mixer and use the whisk attachment to whip together until light and fluffy. This will take about 1-2 minutes. Top the cake with the ricotta icing and compote!

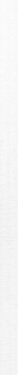

# CASHEW ICE CREAM WITH PEANUT BUTTER & SALTED CARAMEL

I'm obsessed with this combination! As someone who used to work in an ice cream shop, I find it hard to believe that you can get a creamy enough texture from dairy-free ingredients. It turns out, it is possible!

**VEGAN | GF**

**Makes 1.5 litres of ice cream**

360g dried cashews
500ml coconut cream
2 tsp vanilla extract
80g caster sugar
120ml maple syrup
150g peanut butter
40g almond flakes

**For the salted caramel**
80g caster sugar
70ml almond milk
A pinch of sea salt

Prep a baking tray with baking parchment and scoop small spoonfuls of the peanut butter on to the paper. You want these to be bite-size. Place into the freezer for about 30 minutes or until reasonably firm.

To make the caramel, add sugar to a saucepan and place on a medium to high heat. As the sugar starts to melt at the sides, swirl it around the pan. After about 4 minutes you should have a caramel. Remove from the heat. Carefully pour in a little of the milk and use a whisk to quickly beat into the caramel. Allow this to dissolve before adding in a little more. Continue adding in this way until all is combined. Mix in the salt and allow to cool.

Soak cashews in a bowl of newly boiled water for 10 minutes. This should yield 450g soaked cashews when drained but weigh it out.

Add nuts to a high-speed blender along with the coconut cream, vanilla, sugar and maple syrup. Blend until smooth. Then scrape into an ice cream machine and when ready, pour into a 2-litre loaf tin. Mix through the nuts, peanut balls and swirl through the caramel. Make sure the toppings are evenly mixed. Freeze until firm. Take out 15 minutes before serving to soften.

Alternatively, you can freeze the mix straight from the blender. Add to the tin and freeze for 30 minutes before mixing in the toppings. Freeze until firm. This keeps well for 2 weeks.

# BROWN BUTTER BLONDIES

I am very excited to share this recipe as it truly is something special. I made this with my niece and nephew during lockdown and since the IGTV video went up, I have had hundreds of people make them. Let's be honest, brown butter makes most things taste good, but these are a cross between a brownie and a cookie. Definitely try one when it just comes out of the oven. I hope you love them as much as everyone else. A word of advice, try not to sub any of the ingredients so that you get the full experience.

### Makes about 10 blondies

250g unsalted butter
240g light muscovado sugar
2 medium eggs, lightly beaten
2 tbsp maple syrup
2 tsp vanilla extract
1 tsp sea salt
140g spelt flour (or use normal/gluten-free)
120g ground almonds
1 tsp baking powder
100g dark chocolate, roughly chopped
(at least 70% cocoa but I used 85%)

Preheat the oven to 160°C degrees and line an 8-inch square baking tray with baking paper. You can use a rectangle tray but if it is bigger, then just remember the blondies will take less time to cook and be thinner.

Start with the brown butter and melt the butter in a saucepan on a medium to high heat. This will take about 4 minutes. The butter will melt and then start to bubble. Move it around the pan and continue cooking until the butter starts to darken a little and you smell a hazelnut aroma. At this point, quickly remove it from the heat and transfer into a bowl, leaving to cool.

Next mix the flour, ground almonds, baking powder and sea salt into a bowl and mix well.

In another bowl, add the muscovado sugar, eggs, maple syrup and vanilla extract together. Combine well before slowly adding in the slightly cooled brown butter. Mix until you have a nice silky batter. Then stir in the dry ingredients until everything is incorporated. Transfer the mix to the baking tray and lay the uneven pieces of dark chocolate on top. Bake for 35 minutes or until a skin has formed on top. It will be a little gooey inside but that is fine as it will firm up as it cools. Slice into squares and keep sealed in a Tupperware for up to 4 days.

BROWN BUTTER BLONDIES

# CHEESECAKE POTS, BLUEBERRY COMPOTE

My homie, Carolina, who is a cheese fiend, went through a phase of making these for dinner parties. I loved her idea of making these lighter using crème fraîche and she always goes heavy on the vanilla (no bad thing). Grab some good quality granola and you will have these ready for dessert in minutes! You can use mixed nuts and seeds instead of granola.

**GF**

**Makes 6**

360g cream cheese
280ml crème fraîche
60g icing sugar
6 tsp vanilla extract
6 heaped tbsp of gluten-free granola

**For the compote**
150g blueberries
1 tbsp caster sugar
A few drops lemon juice
1 tbsp Grand Marnier

For the compote, place all of the ingredients into a saucepan except the Grand Marnier and simmer for 4 minutes. You just want it to soften and combine into a sauce. Scrape into a bowl and stir in the liquor. Leave to cool.

In a large mixing bowl, add the cream cheese, crème fraîche, icing sugar and vanilla. Use an electric whisk to beat until smooth. This will take 2 minutes. Prep some glasses with the granola divided between them. Spoon in the whipped cream cheese to the pots and top with compote. They last for 3 days covered in the fridge.

# DARK CHOCOLATE VEGAN CAKE

I am seriously into my chocolate so you can rest assured that you will get a proper chocolate hit with every mouthful.

**VEGAN | GF**

**Serves 12**

300g sunflower spread
300g unrefined caster sugar
260g almond flour/ground almonds
70g gluten-free flour
1 level tsp baking powder
¼ tsp bicarbonate of soda powder
80g raw cacao powder/dark coco powder
200ml unsweetened soya yoghurt
6 tbsp almond milk
1 tsp almond extract
3 tsp vanilla extract
Pinch of sea salt

**For the chocolate icing**
210g cashews, soaked overnight
or in newly boiled water for 15 minutes
300ml tinned coconut cream,
stored in the fridge for 1hr
(make sure you weigh out the separated
cream and discard the water)
90g raw cacao powder or
dark coco powder
250g unrefined icing sugar
4 tsp vanilla extract
3 tbsp amaretto
50g freshly grated dark
chocolate for decoration

Preheat oven to 180°C degrees fan and grease two 9 inch cake tins lining with baking parchment. Start by making the cake and add the sunflower spread and sugar into a mixing bowl and use a handheld whisk to cream together for 2-3 minutes until light and fluffy. Weigh the almond flour into a large bowl and add the salt. Sieve in the gluten-free flour, baking powder, bicarbonate soda and cacao powder. Mix together! Then in a smaller bowl stir together the soya yogurt, almond milk, vanilla and almond extract. Carefully add a third of the dry mix to the whipped sunflower oil and sugar until fully incorporated and continue adding a third at a time. Then pour in the yogurt mix and use a wooden spoon to hand mix this until just combined and you should have a smooth thick batter. Do not over mix! Divide between cake tins spreading the batter evenly over to the edges of the tin and bake in the middle of the oven for about 33-35 minutes. The cakes should have risen a little and should be coming away from the sides. A skewer inserted should come out nearly clean and they should be a little springy to touch. Leave to cool completely.

For the icing, drain the cashews from the water and weigh out to 250g. Place nuts into

a blender mixing until they have blended into a paste. This will take about 2-3 minutes and you might need to scrape down the sides. Add the coconut cream along with the rest of the ingredients and blend until just combined. Store icing covered in a cool dry place until needed but not in the fridge. Remove the baking parchment from the cakes and ice both tops before carefully laying one on top of the other. Generously grate over chocolate. I also run a sharp knife over the chocolate to create a few larger flakes. This cake will keep for 2 days.

# APPLE GALETTE,
# SALTED CARAMEL SAUCE

This is inspired by the amazing tarts that you find in the South of France bakeries where they are sticky and are almost burnt a little on top.

**VEGAN**

**Serves 8**

270g plain flour
40g caster sugar
1 tsp cinnamon powder
½ tsp ground cloves
½ tsp ground nutmeg
A pinch of salt
Zest of 1 lemon
1 tsp vanilla extract
120g coconut oil, plus 2 tbsp
extra melted
40ml cold water

2-3 apples (Braeburn are good),
thinly sliced with a mandoline

**For the salted caramel**
240g caster sugar
120ml plant based milk
Big pinch salt

Coconut yoghurt and
a handful of almond flakes
for serving

Preheat oven to 180°C degrees.

Place the first 8 ingredients into a blender or cake mixer with the paddle attachment and mix. Chop up the coconut oil and start adding it a little at a time until it is all incorporated. Then slowly dribble in the water until the dough just comes together. You might not need all of the water. Place dough on an A3 sized sheet of baking paper and lightly dust with flour. Use a rolling pin to roll pastry to 1cm thick and prod with a fork all over a few times. Place onto a baking tray and into the middle of the oven. Bake for 11 minutes and then remove and arrange the thin apple slices on top. You can create 2-3 layers thick of apple slices. Brush the melted coconut oil over the apples and pastry with a pastry brush. Place back into the oven for 8 minutes and then remove.

While the tart is baking you can make the salted caramel. Place sugar into a saucepan and set to a medium to high heat. After about 3 minutes the sugar will start to melt and form a caramel. Every so often, swirl and move the pan around. When the sugar has dissolved, turn off the heat and add a little of the milk. Use a whisk to quickly mix it in. Continue adding a little of the milk at a time until it has all been combined. Add the salt.

When the tart comes out the second time, brush the caramel over the apples and pastry

in a generous layer. You should have over half the caramel leftover for serving. Turn the oven to 200ºC grill fan and place back for 2-3 minutes to caramelise the top. Serve straight away with the caramel.

# VENETIAN GIANDUIOTTO

To visit Venice is to visit a little lagoon paradise. I have been a few times for work and with my family, and every time I discover a new restaurant tucked away under a rickety old bridge or eat my weight in a new gelato flavour. There is a classic gelateria that I go back to time and time again: Nico! Order their iconic Gianduiotto and it arrives on a silver tray with an espresso.

**GF**

**Serves 4, makes 1 litre**

### For the ice cream
500ml double cream
230ml sweetened condensed milk
280g chocolate hazelnut spread
(without palm oil)
4 tsp vanilla extract
1 tsp Grand Marnier

### Chocolate sauce
200ml double cream
60g caster sugar
100g dark chocolate, broken into pieces
1 tsp unsalted butter

### Whipped cream
150ml whipping cream
1 tsp icing sugar

A handful of almond flakes for serving

Add double cream into a mixing bowl and use an electric whisk to beat until it is light and fluffy. Whip in the condensed milk followed by the chocolate spread, vanilla extract and Grand Marnier. When it is well combined, scrape into a plastic container and leave to freeze for about 2 hours or until firm enough to scoop. Take out 15 minutes before serving to allow it to soften.

For the chocolate sauce, add the double cream and sugar into a saucepan and gently heat up until the sugar has dissolved. Let it come to a simmer and then remove from the heat. Place the chocolate into a bowl and pour over the hot cream. Let it sit for 30 seconds before stirring until completely melted together. Mix in the butter.

In a bowl, add whipping cream and icing sugar. Beat together until light and fluffy. Serve the ice cream with whipped cream, a sprinkle of nuts and the sauce on top!

# CHOCOLATE SPELT SHORTBREAD

Spelt flour takes this shortbread to new levels with more flavour and sophistication. It's also all about the quality of the butter and chocolate that you use. There are few ingredients here so try and fork out for a good beurre.

**Makes 12 slices**

180g unsalted butter, at room temperature
200g spelt flour
60g ground almonds
80g caster sugar
A pinch of sea salt
150g dark chocolate (70% cocoa), broken into pieces
1 tsp vanilla extract
A large handful walnuts

Preheat the oven to 190°C degrees. Grease and line a baking tray or 12-inch cake tin with baking parchment.

Add all of the ingredients into a bowl except the walnuts and chocolate and use your hands to mix together into a dough. This shouldn't take long, and then prod the pastry into the baking tray to form a 1.5cm layer. Place into the middle of the hot oven for about 25 minutes or until the top is lightly golden. Leave to cool.

When the shortbread has hardened up, melt the chocolate in a heatproof bowl over a pan of simmering water. Then pour the chocolate over the shortbread and top with crumbled walnuts. Leave to set and you're off! It can be stored in a Tupperware for a few days.

# SPICED POACHED PEAR, COCONUT CREAM

The aromas from the cinnamon, brown sugar and vanilla will fill your kitchen with joy. I love this when pears are in season and it's an incredible fuss-free plant-based dessert.

**VEGAN | GF**

**Serves 2**

2 pears, peeled
1 tin coconut cream (80ml, stored in the fridge for 1 hour)
Handful almond flakes

**For the poaching syrup**
500ml water
150g brown sugar
Cinnamon stick/1 tsp cinnamon
Seeds from 1 vanilla pod/1 tsp vanilla extract
Zest of 1 lemon
1 tbsp Grand Marnier

Add water and brown sugar to a large saucepan and set to a medium to high heat. Heat until sugar has completely dissolved before adding in the cinnamon stick and peeled pears. Using a sharp knife, slice vanilla pod in half lengthways and use the back of the knife to scrape out the seeds. Add seeds and vanilla pod to the saucepan and make a cartouche to sit on top of pears. To make a cartouche, cut a square of greaseproof paper and fold into segments, the shape of an elongated triangle. Trim the triangle to slightly larger than the radius of your pan. Snip 1cm off the sharp point of the triangle and place on top of pears. The little hole should be in the centre of the pan. Bring to boil, and when bubbling, turn down to a simmer for 15-20 minutes or until the pears are cooked all the way through. Remove pears from liquid and discard paper. Add the lemon zest and gently cook liquid to reduce and thicken for another 20 minutes. Then remove from heat and stir in Grand Marnier and place pears back to warm.

Remove coconut cream from the fridge about 15 minutes before serving (this will make it easier to whip). Scoop the thick creamy part out into a bowl and discard the leftover water. Use a whisk to whip up for a 1 minute until a little fluffy. Serve pears in bowls with some of the syrup drizzled over, the coconut cream on top and a sprinkle of almond flakes.

# TAHINI CHOCOLATE COOKIES

What's the sauce in this I hear you say? It is 100 per cent the tahini paste because it's subtle and yet it adds that lil'summin' summin'! Probably the easiest and most delicious cookie you'll ever make!

**VEGAN | GF**

**Recipe makes 10 cookies**

100g almond flour
80g sunflower spread
2 heaped tbsp tahini paste
80g dark chocolate, chopped
95g soft brown dark sugar
30g almond flakes
2 tsp vanilla extract
A pinch of sea salt

Preheat the oven to 170°C degrees and line two baking trays with baking parchment.

Mix together all the ingredients.

Divide the cookie dough between two baking trays lined with baking paper. Leave a 3cm gap between each cookie as the dough spreads in the oven. Bake for 10-12 minutes in a 170°C degree fan oven. Leave to cool and eat up! These will last for about a week in a sealed container.

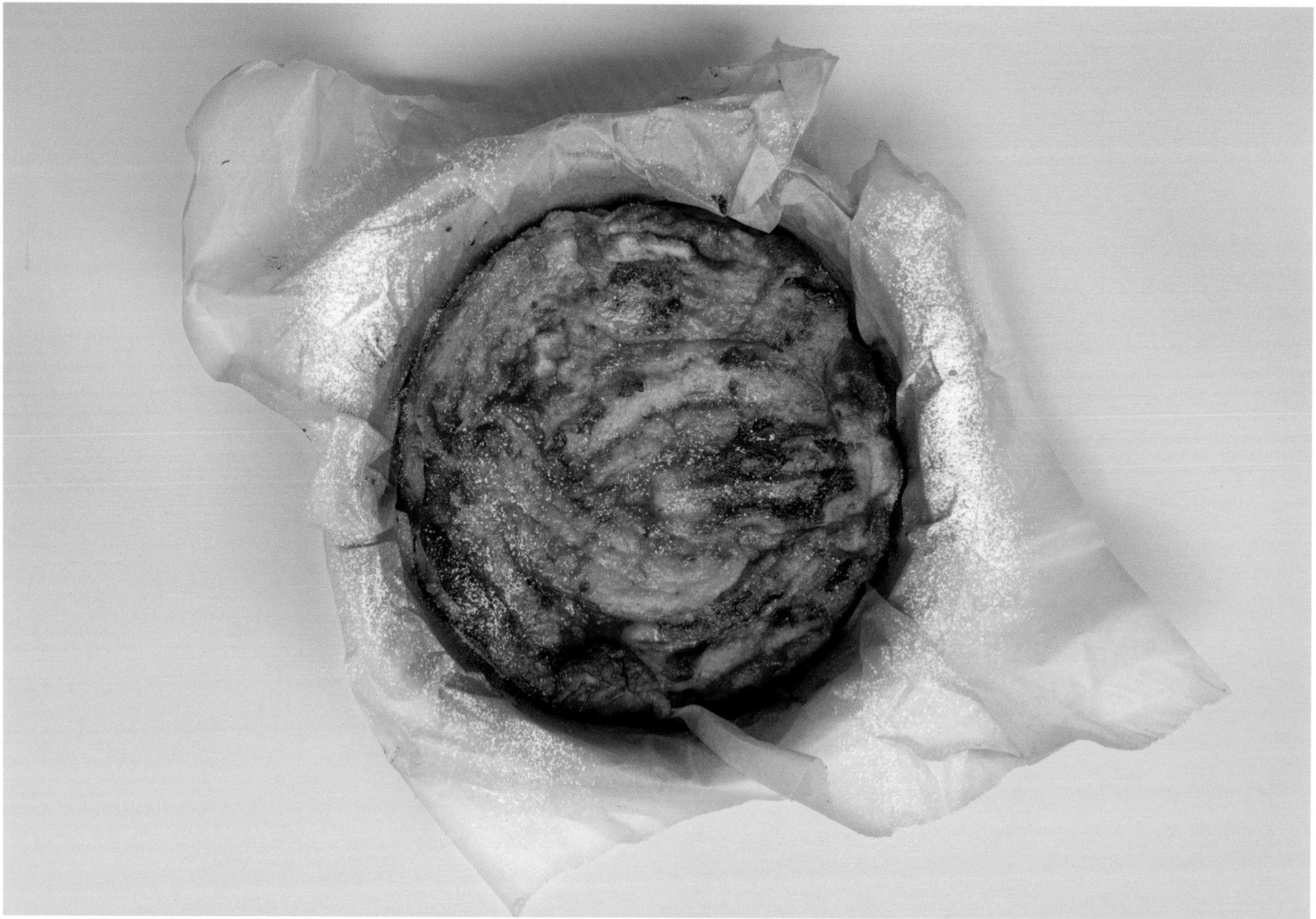

# BROWN BUTTER CLAFOUTIS

This is a French classic and goes well with any berry, but it's traditional to add cherries. Banana really seals the deal for me with the brown butter. This is great for dessert and breakfast.

**Serves 4**

40g unsalted butter
2 bananas, sliced in half and lengthways
2 tbsp spelt flour/plain flour/or blend 2 heaped
tbsp of oats in the blender for oat flour
½ tsp cinnamon powder
1 tsp vanilla extract
Pinch of sea salt
40g caster sugar
2 medium eggs, lightly beaten
160ml whole milk
½ tsp baking powder (if using oat flour)

Preheat the oven to 200°C degrees. Butter and line a 9-inch cake tin or small baking tray with baking parchment.

Add butter to a frying pan and set on a medium to high heat. Melt the butter and stir every few minutes. Gently let it bubble until it starts to colour. This will take about 2-3 minutes and it is ready when gives off a hazelnut smell. At this point, quickly add to a bowl and leave to cool.

In the same pan, add the banana halves, cut side down. Add a pinch of salt and sugar to the pan. Fry for about 1-2 minutes or until they have gone golden. Just cook one side and then carefully add to a plate.

For the batter, add the flour, sugar, cinnamon powder, salt (and baking powder if using) to a bowl and slowly whisk in the beaten eggs. Add a little of the whole milk and beat into the mix until all is incorporated. Then stir in the brown butter and vanilla. You can throw everything into a blender if preferred! Pour into the cake tin and arrange the banana slices cut side up on top. Bake in the oven for 25 minutes or until the batter has puffed right up and the edges have gone golden. Remove and serve with Greek yogurt and a light dusting of icing sugar. This works well with other combinations such as cherries, blueberries, blackberries and chocolate. Also, it's natural for the clafoutis to sink a few minutes after coming out of the oven.

# CARROT CAKE

Here is my vegan version with chopped walnuts and an attempt at a "cream cheese" frosting. You can swap the ground almonds for plain flour but please keep the rest the same. Keep the icing in the fridge until you need it.

**VEGAN**

**Serves 8**

4½ flax eggs (4½ tbsp ground flaxseed and 80ml water (13½ tbsp))
250g caster sugar
90ml sunflower oil (or natural oil)
180g spelt/plain/gluten-free flour
30g ground almonds
¾ tsp baking powder
½ tsp bicarbonate of soda
1½ tsp cinnamon powder
Few gratings of nutmeg
A pinch of salt
1 tsp vanilla extract

150g grated carrots (about 2)
50g walnuts, (30g finely chopped and 20g roughly chopped for the topping)

**For the icing**
250g cashews (soaked in boiling water for 15 minutes or overnight in cold water)
180ml coconut yoghurt
2 tbsp lemon juice
3 tbsp maple syrup
1 tsp vanilla extract

Preheat the oven to 180°C degrees and grease line an 8-inch square/9-inch round cake tin with.

In a small bowl, mix the ground flaxseed and water together and leave to sit for 3 minutes. This will allow it to thicken.

In a large bowl mix the sugar and oil together. In a separate bowl, mix the dry ingredients together (flour, baking powder, bicarb, ground almonds, cinnamon powder, nutmeg and salt). Then add the thickened flax egg in with the oil and sugar followed by the vanilla extract. Next, add in the dry mix and beat until well combined. Then add the grated carrots and 30g walnuts. The batter should be sticky and a little tough. Use a spatula to tip everything into the prepared tin and spread the batter evenly. Bake for 1 hour until a golden top has formed and a skewer inserted comes out nearly clean. Leave to cool completely before icing or cutting.

To make the frosting, drain the cashews and weigh 250g. Add this to a blender along with all the other ingredients for the icing. Blend to a smooth consistency. The mix should come together without adding any more liquid, but you can add 1 tbsp of a plant-based

milk if needed. Be careful not to add loads or your icing will not hold and go too runny. Check the seasoning, adding more lemon juice or maple syrup to taste. Then store in the fridge (1hr) or freezer (20mins) to set.

Ice the cake and top with walnuts. This keeps for 3 days.

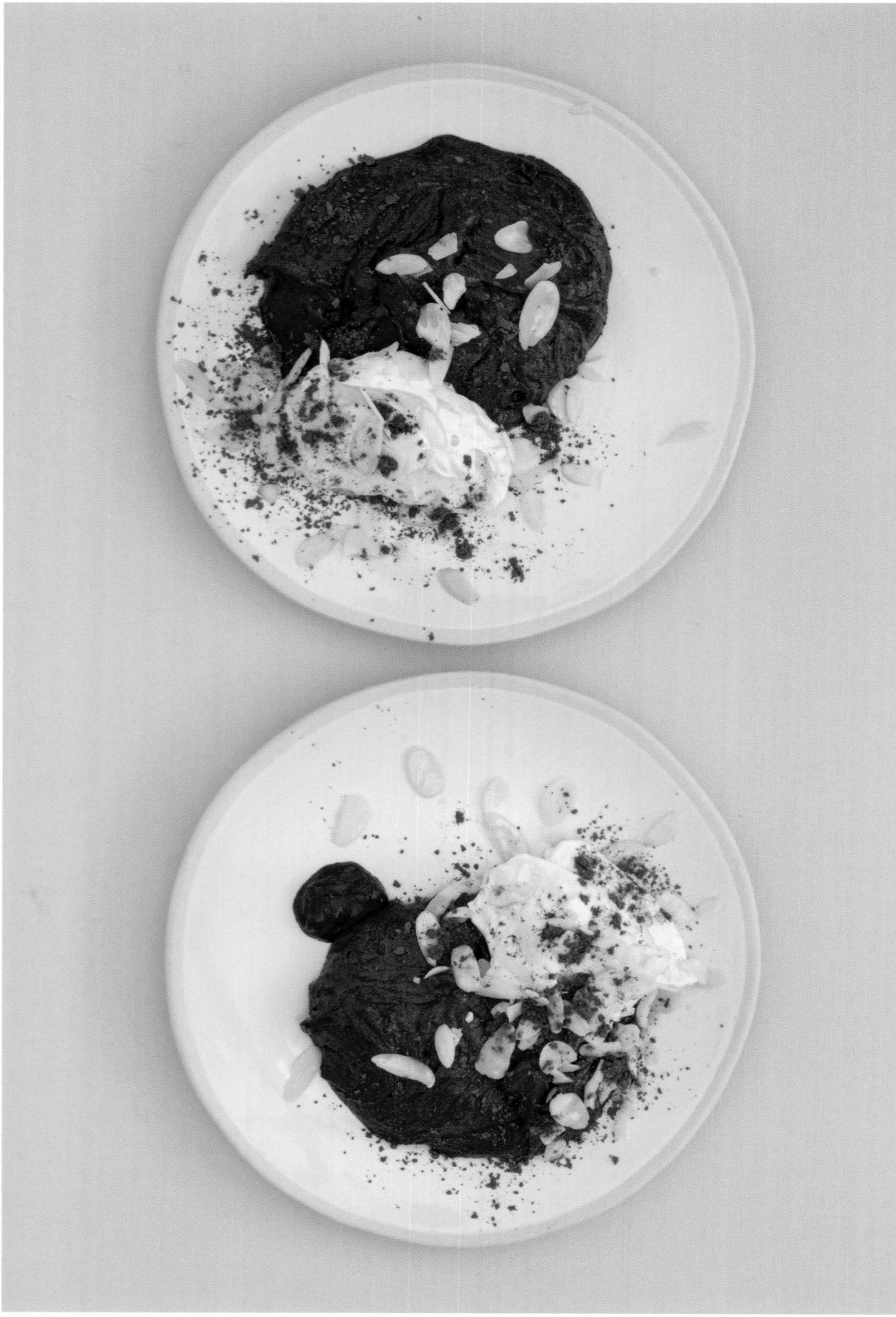

# RAW CACAO CHOCOLATE MOUSSE

I have tried making a raw cacao mousse with avocado and even with frozen banana, neither of which work for me. I just find that the texture is wrong for a chocolate mousse and the banana tends to dominate the other flavours. Here I use coconut cream to give the mousse that creamy texture and you can make this in less than 10 minutes. Raw cacao is extremely bitter, so it needs some sweetness to help balance it out and enhance the taste. I used maple syrup, but you can swap this for date syrup if you prefer. If you are into dark chocolate, then you should be able to wow your dinner party guests with this number and the coconut cream works well to bring lightness to the chocolate.

**VEGAN | GF**

**Serves 2**

**For the mousse**
140ml coconut cream (you will need two 160ml tins that have been chilled in the fridge for a couple of hours)
5 level tbsp raw cacao powder
1 tbsp almond nut butter
1 tsp vanilla extract
4 tbsp maple syrup
1 tsp Grand Marnier/Amaretto (or a tbsp depending on taste)

**For the whipped coconut cream**
100ml coconut cream (you will need two 160ml tins that have been chilled in the fridge for a couple of hours)
1 tsp vanilla extract/bean of half a vanilla pod
5g toasted almond flakes for topping

Add the raw cacao into a blender followed by the rest of the ingredients for the mousse. Blend until all is incorporated and divide between two pots or glasses.

The key with the coconut cream is to use a good quality brand, and to put it in the fridge for two hours or in the freezer for 20 minutes to allow the water and cream to separate. Then you scoop off the thick cream from the top of the tin and leave it to warm up a little so that it can be whipped up easily. I find if it is too cold it doesn't whip properly. In a bowl add the ingredients for the coconut cream and use either an electric or hand whisk to beat until fluffy. This will take about 2 minutes. Spoon this on top of the mousse with a sprinkle of the toasted nuts and serve. You can make this a day ahead and it lasts beautifully.

# BROWN SUGAR RASPBERRY SORBET, COCONUT CREAM

This might be my quickest dessert to date! As long as the raspberries are frozen you can blend it just before dessert and serve it straight away. You can also do this with frozen blueberries and blackberries. Note: the brown sugar and syrup is key to the awesome flavour here!

**VEGAN | GF**

**Makes 1 litre**

500g frozen raspberries
120g soft brown sugar
60ml maple/agave syrup
230ml cold water
1 tsp vanilla extract
A few drops of lemon juice

**For 2 servings**
1 tin coconut cream (160ml, stored in the fridge for 1 hour)
Handful pistachios, roughly chopped

Remove the coconut cream from the fridge about 15 minutes before serving (this will make it easier to whip). Scoop the creamy top and discard the water. Use a whisk to whip up for 1 minute until a little fluffy.

For the sorbet, throw all the ingredients into a high speed blender. Try and use a food processor rather than a tall blender as they tend to mix it in one go. Mix until smooth and then serve straight away with whipped coconut cream and pistachios. You can prep this a few hours before and store in the freezer. Be sure to take it out 15 minutes before you need it to allow it to soften.

# CLASSIC CHOCOLATE CAKE WITH CHOCOLATE BUTTERCREAM

This is the ultimate feel-good chocolate cake and has taken numerous trials to get just right! This would make a great birthday cake and it's got that cakey-cake texture with a luscious indulgent chocolate icing.

**SPELT**

**Serves 8-10**

200g unsalted soft butter, diced
120g caster sugar
100g light muscovado sugar
4 medium eggs (lightly beaten)
100g spelt flour
100g ground almonds
Pinch of salt
1 tsp baking powder
⅓ tsp bicarbonate of soda
60g coco powder
½ tsp instant coffee, sieved

2 tsp vanilla extract
Handful of almond flakes for decoration

**Chocolate Icing**
280g diced unsalted butter
(at room temperature)
100g icing sugar
200g dark choc, chopped
1 tsp vanilla extract
1 tbsp Grand Marnier, optional

Preheat oven to 170°C degrees and butter, line a 9 inch square/8 inch round cake tin with baking parchment.

Use an electric whisk or by hand, beat sugar and butter together for 4-5 mins until light and fluffy. This is important to get a good texture!

Mix flour, ground almonds and salt together. Then sieve in baking powder, bicarbonate of soda, coco powder and instant coffee. Mix until the dry ingredients are well combined. Slowly add a little of the beaten eggs to the creamed butter, followed by a little of the dry ingredients and continue adding in this way until all is incorporated. Stir in vanilla extract and scrape into cake tin. Bake for 35-40 minutes or until a skewer comes out almost clean. Leave to cool completely before slicing in half lengthways. For the icing, melt the chocolate in a heatproof bowl over a saucepan of simmering water. Leave to cool a little.

In a large mixing bowl, beat butter until light and fluffy and then slowly beat in the icing sugar. Add in the vanilla. Slowly beat in the melted chocolate. Divide icing between the two cooled cake halves. Sandwich the cake together. Top with almond flakes. Keeps for 3 days.

# INDEX OF CONTENTS

# THANK YOU

There has been so much time spent writing, trialing, eating, shooting, planning and agonising over this book, and although I might be self-publishing this one, it is by no means a solo effort. To anyone that is thinking of writing your own book, I hope this shows you that with some seriously hard work and determination, it shows that anything is possible. Here is a small thank you to some very, very special people who made it all possible.

Firstly, I want to thank my amazing sister, Juliana who drew the beautiful cover and to her and her husband, Josh who have helped with endless design questions, colours, taglines and late night brainstorming. Thank you for hosting all 6 food shoots at your house and for allowing me to cook in your kitchen whenever I want. You guys are the BEST, I love you and I am forever grateful!

A huge thank you to Kate Metzner for nailing it on the shoots and for being such a great energy to be around. The photos are just as I imagined after our initial insta coffee meeting! To Gail for being the perfect sous chef backstage and for keeping me on track with our record 20 shots in a day.

To Beth McCandlish for taking in my mountain of corrections and endless emails. You have done such a beautiful of job putting it together, thank you! So glad Shaun put us in touch! A big thank you to Shaun Cooper at Taylor Brothers for making this possible and being a total legend. It has been such a pleasure to work with you on this!

To my dad, Tony for being a great proof-reader of over 100 recipes and always being on hand to help, try and critique my cakes:). To my mom, Lydia for being the BEST support and to my brothers Adam and Christian.

I want to say a massive thank you to Milly (@Millykr) for making the whole experience of self publishing less scary and for being incredibly open and kind with all your knowledge. To Emma Lucy-Knowles for giving me that extra push and believing that was all possible. Your vision was very convincing it seems! To my homie, Carolina for basically putting up with me, obrigada. Thank you to my PR, Nadia Walford for jumping on the bandwagon and for helping me while I was probably my most busy and crazy. Muchas gracias to my wonderful agent, Jess for all your work with insta over the last few months. I love working with you! Thank you to my virtual assistant and angel, Annabel for proof-reading and getting the pre-orders going.

Thank you to my friends for putting up with me talking non-stop about this. I love you all! It has been a long and interesting 2020 but hopefully this book will bring a little bit of joy to your kitchen, and of course, sum sauce ;)

**Love, Nina xxxxx**

# SAUCY PLAYLIST

---

What makes cooking and spending time in the kitchen even better? Music! I have put together over 10 hours of music and I am hoping that there is something for everyone. It starts chilled with mellow guitar vibes, followed by soul to indie to gentle rock and flows on to some hip hop and salsa.

Then, once the sauce is truly bubbling, we go into some jungle, disco and electro. So crack open a bottle and have a dance on me!

To access the playlist, open the Spotify app and go to the search icon and tap in the search finder. At the top right corner, the camera icon should appear and then scan the barcode to access the music.

Bon appétit!